Alistair McDowall

Plays: 2

X: 'McDowall masterfully plants ideas that grow until they explode into extraordinary shapes. Filthy humour breaks down into a cracked algorithm of letters and loss ... a play that will gnaw away at you.' *The Stage*

The Glow: 'A mind-bending, ambitious play, which attempts impossible things, demonstrating the power of theatre to bridge the gap between imagination and reality.' *Exeunt*

all of it: 'Genius...an epic of inner life...McDowall brilliantly captures how febrile consciousness scribbles around our spoken half-truths.' *Guardian*

Northleigh, 1940: 'Quietly devastating...[McDowall] is extraordinary at channelling his disturbing, poetic vision of the characters' hidden worlds.' *The Times*

Zero for the Young Dudes! A play for youth groups commissioned by the National Theatre and performed around the country in 2017.

Alistair McDowall grew up in the North East of England. Plays include: *all of it* (2023) (Royal Court Theatre/Avignon Festival 2023), *The Glow* (Royal Court Theatre 2022); *all of it* (Royal Court Theatre 2020); *Zero for the Young Dudes!* (National Theatre Connections 2017); *X* (Royal Court Theatre 2016); *Pomona* (RWCMD/Gate 2014; Orange Tree Theatre/Royal Exchange/National Theatre 2014/5); *Talk Show* (Royal Court Theatre 2013); *Brilliant Adventures* (Royal Court Young Writers' Festival 2012; Royal Exchange, Manchester and Live Theatre, Newcastle 2013) and *Captain Amazing* (Live Theatre, Newcastle and Edinburgh Fringe 2013; UK tour 2014). He is a MacDowell fellow, and a recipient of the Harold Pinter Commission. His work has been translated and produced internationally.

ALISTAIR MCDOWALL

Plays: 2

X
The Glow
all of it
Northleigh, 1940
Zero for the Young Dudes!

with an introduction by Vicky Featherstone

methuen | drama

METHUEN DRAMA
Bloomsbury Publishing Plc
50 Bedford Square, London, WC1B 3DP, UK
1359 Broadway, New York, NY 10018, USA
29 Earlsfort Terrace, Dublin 2, Ireland

BLOOMSBURY, METHUEN DRAMA and the Methuen Drama logo are trademarks of Bloomsbury Publishing Plc

First published in Great Britain 2025
X © Alistair McDowall, 2016
The Glow © Alistair McDowall, 2022
all of it © Alistair McDowall, 2023
Northleigh, 1940 © Alistair McDowall, 2023
Zero for the Young Dudes! © Alistair McDowall, 2017

Alistair McDowall has asserted his right under the Copyright, Designs and Patents Act, 1988, to be identified as author of this work.

For legal purposes the Acknowledgements on p. iv constitute an extension of this copyright page.

Cover image © Craig Stewart | craigstewart.studio

All rights reserved. No part of this publication may be: i) reproduced or transmitted in any form, electronic or mechanical, including photocopying, recording or by means of any information storage or retrieval system without prior permission in writing from the publishers; or ii) used or reproduced in any way for the training, development or operation of artificial intelligence (AI) technologies, including generative AI technologies. The rights holders expressly reserve this publication from the text and data mining exception as per Article 4(3) of the Digital Single Market Directive (EU) 2019/790.

Bloomsbury Publishing Plc does not have any control over, or responsibility for, any third-party websites referred to or in this book. All internet addresses given in this book were correct at the time of going to press. The author and publisher regret any inconvenience caused if addresses have changed or sites have ceased to exist, but can accept no responsibility for any such changes.

No rights in incidental music or songs contained in the work are hereby granted and performance rights for any performance/presentation whatsoever must be obtained from the respective copyright owners.

All rights whatsoever in this play are strictly reserved and application for performance etc. should be made before rehearsals by professionals and by amateurs to Blue Posts Management Limited (www.bluepostsmanagement.com). No performance may be given unless a licence has been obtained.

A catalogue record for this book is available from the British Library.
A catalog record for this book is available from the Library of Congress.

ISBN: PB: 978-1-3505-4740-7
ePDF: 978-1-3505-4742-1
eBook: 978-1-3505-4741-4

Series: Contemporary Dramatists

Typeset by Newgen KnowledgeWorks Pvt. Ltd., Chennai, India
Printed and bound in Great Britain

For product safety related questions contact productsafety@bloomsbury.com.

To find out more about our authors and books visit www.bloomsbury.com and sign up for our newsletters.

Contents

Introduction by Vicky Featherstone vii
Preface by the author xv
X 1
The Glow 161
all of it 263
Northleigh, 1940 311
Zero for the Young Dudes! 329

Introduction

X
The Glow
all of it
Northleigh, 1940
Zero for the Young Dudes!

Looking back at these plays, it is both comforting and inspiring to know there is nothing I can write, which can get close to conveying the originality, audacity, fearlessness, purity of vision and utter trust in the medium of theatre to express what must be expressed, as is here in these pages.

With these five plays in one place, it is an opportunity to delve deep into the heart of Ali's work. It is an invitation for you as readers – and hopefully potential makers – of the plays, to immerse yourselves in the ideas, the forms, the language, and explore what Ali perceives it is to be human in these times.

As ever with a rigorous and intelligent writer, the answers you seek will actually be in the writing. In rehearsal Ali would tell us what he had been listening to when he wrote a certain section or which poem, film, or novel had stimulated something in his thinking, but he never gave us any answers. We would explore and strive and try to understand. A never-ending but deeply rewarding process.

According to Ali, I 'commissioned 2 of them, directed 3 of them, was the first reader and a co-pilot on the 4th, and ran the NT Connections workshop for the last'.

That I even got to read and subsequently meet Ali is down to Chris Campbell, the then Literary Manager at the Royal Court. During my first few days at the Court as AD in 2013, Chris Campbell put *Talk Show* on my desk for me to read (Ali had written it as part of the writers group run by Leo Butler). I met with Ali to tell him we were going to put it on as part of our Open Court Repertory season in the summer of 2013. And so began our now twelve-year conversation.

Ali said of *Talk Show* at the time that he felt it to be the most personal of his plays, but it is clear he could have no notion of what he would go on to write.

Talk Show was about men not able to express their emotions well – if at all. In Ali's introduction to the first volume of his plays, he writes about *Talk Show* and two others: 'They're all preoccupied with what happens when women leave the picture'.

The plays in this volume however are all exclusively women-led stories – apart from *Zero for the Young Dudes!* which was a specific NT connections commission for young people and has no gender assigned to any of the lines or characters – although interestingly he does put 'she' in some of the stage directions...

Several times I have been asked – and I know Ali has too – about his choice of writing these extraordinary parts for women. Questioning both his right to do so, but more interestingly about how deeply felt and brilliantly true they are. It is not for a writer to explain why they write what they write, but for me it is interesting. The men in the plays have often reached the limits of their emotional ability, something of which they are often painfully aware – they end up reminded of their mortality, becoming frail or ill and in *X* literally ending up in the freezer.

The women however – suffering under the constraints and limitations put upon them by the different societies or times they live in, seek to escape.

Mrs Lyall in *The Glow* expresses this most lucidly, in her quest to become a medium and overcome the patriarchal oppressions and pettiness which surround her, but others – like Gilda and Mattie in *X*, and the central women in *The Glow* and *Northleigh, 1940* – literally transcend our corporeal world and in their different ways become one with the universe. Ali is never writing to express the experience of being a woman, more to investigate the paradox between how we are seen and treated in the world and what power he sees we actually hold.

The worlds of superheroes (*Captain Amazing*) and talk shows which play a game with their audience seem to me the beautiful concerns of a boyish, youthful mind, but in these subsequent plays, things mature into much more complex universes, wrestling with all of history, evolution, time, space, ecology, humanity and language. It is the difference between the corporeal and the immaterial or spiritual.

All the plays here are entirely unique from each other – inhabiting very different imaginative worlds to hold the stories – all have a completely different set of production and acting provocations, but having them in a volume encourages us to look at them as a body of work and so here we can look at what connects them.

These plays look outwards and upwards beyond our immediate world, but as they do, they also become more deeply focused and unafraid of the internal worlds of the central characters. Internal worlds are to be fiercely protected and admired, as the protagonist scorns in *Northleigh, 1940*:

She didn't think her mother had ever had an internal life.

They travel constantly between the hugely epic and the intimately personal, and among other things it is in experiments with language that Ali explores and communicates that.

Language becomes a conscious tool starting, ironically, with the complete obliteration of it in *X*.

The crew of a research base on Pluto have been abandoned by their colleagues on earth. We grow to understand that Earth is probably not even there as we knew it and we have ignored the signs of its collapse – the last tree, the end of birdsong – as Ray says:

Earth is pissing its last and everyone is just looking at their fucking shoes.

As they lose their grip a kind of eco-homesickness takes over, as memories of Earth and the past lives of the characters fade, everything starts to disintegrate until language itself collapses and Gilda and Clark, who are still trying to keep the words for things alive – the bird, the story of the tree, their own names – are literally left in a void, with nothing but *XXXXXXX* to say to each other.

When I first read *X* and we committed to doing it, to be honest, I was unsure the *X* pages would survive. I believed I understood them, and my thought was that we would go for it in rehearsal and see what we discovered, but then I would probably have to negotiate with Ali that they didn't earn their place; they were indulgent and would turn audiences away – alienating them from what I thought was the play.

The day we got to them in rehearsals and the actors just jumped in and went there was eye-opening. Everything in the play had built up to that moment where the breakdown was inevitable and the void was terrifying and very real. Repeatedly in these plays, Ali builds to heightened explosions of symbiosis with form, idea, character and story and it transcends the logical to exist on a visceral and emotional level.

Ultimately the only thing which always survives is love – both the new-found love which Clark and Gilda finally have for each other and then the fierce maternal love for Mattie, who is born after nine desperately lonely and horror-filled months for Gilda. Love, and in particular maternal love, sits profoundly at the heart of many of Ali's plays, and *X* ends with the comfort of a creation story, begged for by both Young Mattie and older Mattie with the simple question:

What was your mum like?

The dying Gilda tells the story of her mother – the last tree – and how she was lifted here to remember the rest. By repeating and holding on to our story we know we are still alive.

In *The Glow*, Ali brings to life the silent woman who is present at the edges in so much Western art and literature. He sends her throughout time as a vessel, knowing nothing of herself. The structure of the play means that the woman learns who she is as we move forwards, even though we go back and forth in time – she initially learns to speak, finding her voice and words in front of us, then learns to read, and in doing so what the glow – her power – means, but most of all she seeks a name.

She is finally given the gift of one – Brooke – and also an unlikely home by the previously hate-filled Haster.

The fear of not having a name – of being dehumanized – also exists in *X* when at Clark's lowest moment he panics as he has forgotten his name – *we can have new names* comforts Gilda, and he chooses Kratos from a video game. The names seem vital to each character but totally unimportant and oddly unpoetic in the scope of the plays as ultimately they become bodies in the universe, or matter existing as stars – both terrifying and comforting at the same time.

This is made most clear in the speech at the end of *The Glow*.

Although using largely naturalistic language throughout, it is in the creation myth at the end of the play which swells into a beautiful verse speech, unlocking a more conscious use of language and form to express the truly epic scale of the woman's story. It tells the story of her evolution, the development of the sentient being and community, the destruction of the world in our search for meaning, and then as the woman is picked up in a solar flare and becomes the stars, she has the chance to begin again, with all knowledge and experience in her breath, to start something new – if she so desires.

I was taken aback and thrilled by the poetic, roiling language when I first read it, but was nervous about how it would work. It's a huge ask after the complex story and world of *The Glow*, both for performer and for the audience, but I was wrong again – the heightened language which in rehearsal we wrestled with, was, Ali said, a reclaiming from the classical and was entirely appropriate for a woman who had not had anything, not even language or a name, to get to take that space and to elevate and communicate another dimension in her understanding of herself.

There are chapters to be written about grief, loneliness and loss in these plays: The Woman realizing she is the only one and there are no others, and returning to the cave without Haster; Ellen wracked with sadness at the loss of Evan and because of the love she showed to The Woman, being given the chance to see him once more; Mattie alone forever in space having lost Gilda, who in turn has mourned her mother, the last tree; and in *Northleigh, 1940*, where although the protagonist did not have a good relationship with her mother at all, she has been unable to communicate with her dad since her death, so much so she lies about what time she starts work so as not to share the same bus. But throughout I always feel the plays are reminding me to not obliterate what is good, and to carry the love and hope and learning into the new futures even though – *the past is always with us,* as Evan tells The Woman.

Northleigh, 1940, inspired by the census of all the inhabitants of the house Ali was living in during lockdown, is the story of an aspiring young writer who works as a secretary and shares the house with her dad after the death of her mum.

On my first read, I sighed quietly that it started in the same register as the end of *The Glow*, but was quickly and joyfully wrongfooted when the character interrupts her own train of story-thought with the notion of buying a gramophone for her bedroom. As the piece progresses you are given the option to think this opener is now probably relegated to the kind of literature she enjoys – *the crude illustrations of tentacled monsters on the cover*. At the end of the piece as the bomb drops on the father and daughter in their Morrison shelter, Ali creates another new language form, less florally poetic, but with real imagistic precision mirroring the pace of the bomb dropping and the obliteration of all it is about to hit.

all of it feels like the quintessence of all of these.

Ali wrote this over just three nights while on a writing retreat in the United States. He was struggling with *The Glow* which was taking draft upon draft and a huge host of characters (which do not speak in the final version) to bring it to life, and writing *all of it* was solace for him. When he returned home, he brought me the play in an envelope and left it with me to read. This is the play out of all of them which speaks most for itself. It is a true work of art – outstanding in its shape, arc, rhythm, humour, storytelling and recognizability. It's life-affirming and desperately sad and for me encompasses all of the work in the one hit.

Oddly it is the most ordinary of Ali's plays – with nothing exceptional really happening – other than the whole of a life.

It starts with a baby girl being born, literally pushing herself out of the birth canal, and charts in minute detail over the course of the next 40 minutes an entire life well-lived. She learns to speak, goes to school, has a baby brother, friendships and friendship anxiety, her first kiss, loses her virginity, goes to university, falls in love, gets a job.

There is a huge playfulness and ease with language – the *driving to work, driving to work* section, the intrusive thoughts of *everyone dies* as she learns about death, the woman who tentatively has said throughout her life that she wants to be a poet, finally at a poetry event and all she says is *POEM.*

Life and death loom large, and as mentioned before there is grief and loneliness, but it is the cycle of death and birth here that carries the ache of existence so incredibly and shapes the piece – the shock and effect on her and her brother of her Mum dying when she is at university, and then the joy of her own daughter and her granddaughter being born, and finally her own approach to death, all however shadowed by the suicide of her brother which she can never forgive herself for.

Every time we have done this play or I reread it or use it for a workshop it takes me aback. That a piece of writing like this could so encapsulate whole scenes, periods of life, moments of love, sex, joy, pain in such vivid detail with some unusual spacing on the page and a few words seems like alchemy.

Its power is in the accumulation of an entire life which goes just as swiftly as it came, and in those final moments you feel an unbelievable sense of loss – a pain and a grief so great, at the speed of it all and the vast smallness of it all. It really is a masterpiece.

Zero for the Young Dudes! I can't write about this play with as personal a lens as the others. This play sits slightly outside the other four as it is a specific commission for a specific purpose, but it knows its audience and cast and is a provocation of staging and form. It invites the company to investigate it thoroughly in order to be able to perform it – it requires a negotiation and a collaboration to decide who says what and how it will look and be delivered. The title speaks brilliantly and tragically for itself. It offers a radical view of a dystopian world, and is an invitation to the youth not to accept the shit which the elders are continually handing on to them with no mind for their futures – a huge theme in *X* of course. The double invitation of theatrical discovery and radical revolution for the youth is enticing and generous.

In our constant human attempt to understand ourselves, to define ourselves through our story (Haster, in *The Glow – all a man wants is to become a story. To persist.*) there is a striving and a yearning in these plays which we recognize. A fundamental ache about the beauty of love and the transience of life and the infinite loss that experiencing such love will bring, but that we must never shy away from. As Ellen says at the end of *The Glow – the joy of knowing him was greater than the pain of losing him.*

Writing this foreword at the very end of 2024, I think about where Ali could possibly take us next and I look to his writing for the glimmer of a suggestion.

Even after all she has been through, at the end of *The Glow* as The Woman holds the light, there is hope and love, and as Ellen has said to her, the chance of something new:

And know this spark might come to life anew-
Should I choose to ignite it with a breath.
This light and I. Alone. Together.
And I think of her.
And what she told me.
And I cradle the glow.
And wait.
And wonder.

We wait and wonder, Ali.
XO

Preface

The question most often asked about a play is some variation of: Where did it come from? Or: Where did you get the idea?

I have never managed an answer to this that's satisfied anyone asking the question.

If I could explain where they came from, I wouldn't have had to write them in the first place. Years later, once the play has been produced a few times, I can usually be a little more articulate as to what the play is, and where it might have come from, but it remains guesswork.

Yet here I am attempting to write an introduction, despite having little to say about where each of these plays came from originally. But I've always enjoyed these introductions myself, and, particularly when I was younger, found them helpful in how they demystified the process of writing. So I'm going to attempt to gather a few thoughts about each one, leaning more towards the practical process of writing them, in the hope that some of these vague memories might be of at least minor interest to any writers reading this.

All of these plays (bar one, uncharacteristically) were difficult to write, on a sliding scale from 'Really Very Hard' to 'Complete Fucking Nightmare'. I get a kind of fulfilment from writing that I get from very little else, but it's a difficult, hard-won fulfilment. One that comes from building something that wasn't there before, against the odds. There are moments writing when I achieve a strange euphoria unlike anything else, when something locks in and I solve something I've been struggling with. But much of the time it's just very hard.

A number of the plays here I had to start again from scratch—multiple times. All of the plays here I had to talk myself into not throwing away. This, in fact, makes up much of my process: an elaborate series of self-deceptions and pep talks to myself that what I'm doing is worth continuing with. One needs to muster a lot of self-belief to write. While I have belief in my abilities, my belief in the play while writing it hangs on very tenuous threads for a significant part of the process. This is likely in part because of how amorphous they are at first. How, once dredged up from wherever it is they come from, they will resemble nothing much to anyone but myself for a long time. To attempt to explain what the play is going to be at that point would be like trying to explain what a jellyfish is in a foreign language.

X

X *was a commission for the Royal Court. I got extremely stuck with it almost immediately.*

I knew the play was about a mother and her daughter, and a goodbye of some sort. I knew the mother was called Gilda. I spent months trying and failing to write this play. In the end I got so hacked off with it I put it in a drawer and started noodling around with another play that had arrived in my head – an odd thing about a group of people stuck on Pluto gradually losing all sense of time. Very quickly I realized they were the same play. I'm sure I've said this elsewhere – likely in another introduction I am now replicating – but plays often seem to come when two things I'd thought were separate reveal themselves to be the same. So it was with this play. The various wants and fears and metaphors of the two ideas locked in with each other when I put them together. It seems obvious in retrospect: losing someone you love might well feel like being stranded on another planet.

I struggled repeatedly with the fact it was set on Pluto – I was convinced the Royal Court would tell me to piss off should I hand this in. This turned out to be a good thing for the writing of it, as I worked to ground the play as much as possible. It's often termed (understandably) a science-fiction play, but it's never seemed like that to me. It was a play much more inspired by David Storey's work plays and The Cherry Orchard *than it was by* 2001. *In rehearsal we often talked about* Terms of Endearment *or Conor McPherson's plays.*

X *seems like a play of two halves, but – and this is partly why it was so difficult to write – both halves are actually doing the same thing, it's just hidden in the first half. I am still reluctant to point out the specifics of what that 'same thing' is.*

The Glow

The Glow *was commissioned soon after* X – *I started writing it in autumn of 2016, and it opened at the Royal Court in 2022. Over those years I rewrote the play endlessly, often from scratch – quite literally picking up a blank page and pen and starting again. It's without doubt the play of mine that I had the most difficulty writing, and came following a period of falling fairly comprehensively out of love with the theatre. This has happened again since, and I think is more than likely down to my desperation to never repeat myself – I want the next play to be completely new in both content and form, and this pressure I put on myself sends me into a desert where I can't think of anything I want to do, nor find much in the way of guideposts that might help me head in that direction.*

The only theatre I took solace in during that time was on YouTube: the RSC's 1980 production of Nicolas Nickleby, *adapted by David Edgar and Trevor Nunn; and Philip Glass and Robert Wilson's opera* Einstein on the Beach. *So looking at the play now it's not a huge surprise that much of its tone resides in an odd blend of old-fashioned, Dickensian storytelling via multi-roling, and a more abstract relationship with light and dark as arenas for both sensation and meaning.*

It took me so long to write mainly because I had the form wrong for so long. It's a story about a woman who, we discover in the second act, is immortal. Most of my initial attempts to write the play were my trying and failing to write just about everything she experienced, and pack the play with every character she met. I thought I was writing a symphony, when in reality the play wanted to be a chamber piece. Once I'd figured this out things became a lot easier – leaning into the looping and repeating of themes and characters.

The first draft would have run about eight hours long, though there's not much in it that didn't make it to the final version – it's just here in glances, or half a line, or an image that disappears as quickly as it appeared.

I managed, for the original publication of the play, to get an academic to write an afterword about the play's sources. Unfortunately she's declined to have it reprinted – if you'd like to read more about 'The Woman in Time' you'll have to seek the original text out.

all of it/Northleigh, 1940

I wrote all of it *in a cabin in the woods in New Hampshire, USA, a very short walk from where Thornton Wilder wrote* Our Town. *While writing* The Glow *I'd had an awful moment of realization – that the rest of my life might be like this: sitting at a desk feeling quite depressed while trying to write something very difficult, rarely seeing other people, or even sunlight. In an act of desperation I applied to go to the MacDowell writer's retreat – where* Our Town *was written. I reasoned that even if I wrote nothing I could have a Wilder pilgrimage.*

But in the end I read almost exclusively poetry while there – in part because I'd spent the last decade reading so many plays that I'd burnt myself out to a degree, and also because I felt with The Glow *I'd come to the end of a certain road I'd been travelling for a while. I'd written three plays* (Pomona, X, The Glow) *that all had very elastic narratives, and were fixated on finding more and more gymnastic structures to stretch those narratives around. By the end of* The Glow *I wanted to start from scratch and just think about words.*

While I was at MacDowell there were a lot of poets there, and so I spent my evenings talking about Emily Dickinson and Wallace Stevens with people who knew much more about them than me. So it makes sense that following a period of reading poetry more seriously, the next play that arrived was leaning more into that realm – the words in all of it *are selected as much for their sound and rhythm and colour as they are the meanings we've given them. It's a play with a very conventional structure, but with an acrobatic approach to language.*

I wrote it across three evenings and barely changed a word before it opened in spring 2019. This is a terrible brag, but I don't think it'll happen again, and I'm sharing it here out of fear that the rest of this introduction has been quite downbeat about the process of writing – sometimes you get lucky.

I managed to get Kate O'Flynn to do all of it *– I'd always wanted to work with her, and once I had, I just wanted to work with her more. Her technical ability is astonishing, and so it was enormous* *fun to write two more pieces for her, knowing that I was unlikely to find her limits no matter how far I pushed things.*

In Stereo was the second, and due to its formatting, we couldn't reprint it here (it's available in the wider, more square collection Three Poems *– which remains the "definitive" printing of these three plays as it preserves all my line breaks.). The third was* Northleigh, 1940, *so named for the road I lived on from 2016 to 2021, featuring characters named after those I found listed in the 1940 census of the area.*

All three plays have a strange relationship with the notion of character – neither fully inhabiting nor disposing of it, sitting in a strange liminal space in between. This follows on from The Glow, *which has an oddly similar approach to character, despite seeming much more conventional on the surface. In* Northleigh, *the play itself seems to orbit the central character – never quite allowing the actor to fully inhabit her in the traditional sense. Just as they finally do, we are snatched away into the sky.*

Zero for the Young Dudes!

Zero... *was written for the National Theatre's Connections programme before the rest of these plays – or at least, in between the two acts of* X. *I've put it at the end as it sits slightly outside the others in a couple of ways, but mostly because the long title it's lumbered with looked neater listed as the last on the cover.*

The title comes from two sources that inform the play to varying degrees: the most obvious being the Mott the Hoople song, the more obscure being Jean Vigo's 1933 short film Zero for Conduct, *about pupils at a boarding school revolting against the teachers.*

National Theatre Connections is one of the most important, meaningful contributions the theatre industry makes to the nation at large. Ten or so playwrights are commissioned to write plays to be sent out to scores of drama groups up and down the country – each picks the play they want to do, then produce it.

It's a tricky commission as you've no idea how many you're writing for – it will likely be a lot, but could be fewer than you'd guess, so ideally you need to write something flexible. I remember struggling with the play until I decided to lean more heavily into the strictures – I wrote something that could be done with five or fifty actors. I'm always so pleased when I hear another group are doing it – I still remember what it meant to me being in plays at school.

Drama as a subject has been constantly under attack for the last decade or so. There's an assumption that it's a luxury subject, or a doss. The things I learned doing drama in the tiny mobile classroom at Stokesley School, just outside Middlesbrough, have eclipsed much of what I took from my other subjects – and not because I now work as a playwright. Because the fundamentals of Drama as a school subject – empathy, trust, patience, curiosity, improvisation and experiment – are all aspects that add up to becoming a well-rounded human.

The main thing I feel about these plays now is a huge sense of gratitude I got to write them and have them produced, and a hope that I get to make more. Nothing's a given – at the time of writing this I'm in the process of finally breaking a period without writing that followed the sudden loss of my mother. It's not something that's talked about enough amongst writers – or artists of any kind, for that matter – that when something that enormous happens, it knocks you off your axis in a way that makes it very difficult to work the same way you did before. A loss like that rewires your brain, and it's been taking me some time to figure out the new wiring and how to work with it.

Especially since, in every play here, my mother feels very present.

Thank you to Anthony Banks, who commissioned Zero...*, and Vicky Featherstone, who commissioned the rest and directed almost all of them, teaching me endless things about plays in the process.*

Thanks to Sam Pritchard, who directed Northleigh *and was also an extra voice of encouragement during* The Glow's *awkward labour.*

Thanks to every writer I worked with as a member of the many groups I ran at the Royal Court between 2015 and 2023, the years these plays were coming into being; the conversations we had about writing, art and life contributed to these plays in countless ways.

Thanks to Chris Campbell,
Thanks to Alice Birch and Rory Mullarkey,
Thanks to Howard Gooding,
Thanks to Amy,
Thanks to you for picking up this book.

Alistair McDowall,
2024.

X

for mum.

X was first performed at the Royal Court Jerwood Theatre Downstairs, Sloane Square, on Wednesday 30 March 2016, with the following cast and creative team:

Cole Rudi Dharmalingam
Young Mattie Grace Doherty/Amber Fernée
Ray Darrell D'Silva
Clark James Harkness
Gilda Jessica Raine
Mattie Ria Zmitrowicz

Director Vicky Featherstone
Designer Merle Hensel
Lighting Designer Lee Curran
Composer & Sound Designer Nick Powell
Video Designer Tal Rosner
Assistant Director Roy Alexander Weise

Characters

Gilda
Mattie
Clark
Cole
Ray

Notes

A question without a question mark denotes a flatness of tone.

– Indicates an interruption of speech or train of thought.

. . . Indicates either a trailing off, a breather, a shift, or a transition.

/ Indicates where the next line of dialogue interrupts or overlaps.

Act One

I.

A small research base on Pluto.

We're in the communal room, which has a table/chairs.

Open exits leading off left and right.

A ladder leading up through an open access hatch above.

A kitchen unit on the back wall.

Above that, a large, circular window that looks out into blackness.

Above that, a large digital clock displaying the time.

It resembles an airport waiting room. Or an expanded train carriage.

Functional and charmless.

It's slightly untidy and cluttered.

It's late.

Gilda *stands,* **Ray** *sits and eats.*

Silence.

Gilda   . . . it's not so long.

Ray   It's long.

Pause.

Ray   It's a long time.

Pause.

Gilda There was that time – Before, we lost them –

Ray That's / not –

Gilda We had nothing from them then –

Ray They warned us before, we knew that was going to happen, it was *scheduled*.

They were repairing a satellite.

Gilda Maybe they're doing that now.

Ray It's completely different.

Gilda It might just be –

Ray Two days with prior warning is completely different to three *weeks* radio silence.

. . .

If someone farts out here they want to know about it.

They want a ten-page report on who farted, when they farted, *why* they farted.

You're *Miss* Paperwork for fuck's sake.

That's half the reason they keep us locked to their hours, so they can breathe down our necks easier.

And I've been out here a thousand times and haven't / *once* –

Gilda Not this far.

Ray It doesn't matter –

Gilda *No one's* been out this far –

Ray Three weeks, no contact, that is a long time. Wherever you are.

. . .

That is a problem.

. . .

It's not something to debate.

Pause.

Gilda *goes to the cupboard and retrieves a box of cereal.*

She eats a handful.

Pause.

Gilda So then we go through all the systems –

Ray He says they're fine.

Gilda So then one of the satellites –

Ray He says they're fine.

Gilda If it was fine we'd be talking to them, something is not fine –

Ray He says everything tech-wise is.

Gilda There's *something* wrong –

Ray Of course there's something wrong but it's outside his range of influence.

Gilda His range of influence?

Ray Calm down. It's late.

Gilda You're telling me to panic –

Ray I'm telling you how it is.

You're a grown woman, calm down.

Beat.

Gilda I don't like how you talk to me.

Ray Well.

He takes some pills from a bottle in his pocket.

Gilda What are those.

Ray Pills.

Gilda What pills?

Ray My pills, it's none of your business what pills, why would I tell you what / pills I take?

Gilda I'm sorry –

. . .

Sorry.

Pause.

Gilda So what do we do.

Pause.

Gilda What can we do?

Ray Nothing.

Gilda Noth –

Ray There's nothing *to* do. We wait.

Gilda We can't just –

Ray We're here, they're there.

Gilda I get that –

Ray The phone lines are fucked.

Gilda Yes –

Ray We can't reach them, they can't reach us.

Gilda No –

Ray They're supposed to have picked us up by now –

Gilda We don't –

Ray And we've no means of going anywhere ourselves –

Gilda I know –

Ray So then what are you asking me for?

What do you think I know that you don't?

You're the genius here, why don't you tell *me* what to do?

Beat.

She blinks.

Oh Jesus Christ.

Gilda What.

Ray I can't even have a normal conversation –

You're supposed to be my second in command.

Gilda I'm *fine* –

Ray I can't talk to you if you're going to start blubbing every / time –

Gilda I'm not 'blubbing'.

Ray Well it looks like you're doing something.

Gilda I'm not.

...

But if I was,

Which I'm not,

But if I was it would be a perfectly appropriate response to the situation.

Pause.

Ray They will come and get us.

Maybe they're late, maybe something's wrong, but they'll come.

...

And not because of us, but because you don't send billions' worth of gear to Pluto then forget about it.

...

We've done eighteen months. A few more won't kill us.

Pause.

Gilda I wasn't crying.

II.

There's a large X smeared across one of the walls in thick, faded brown strokes.

Clark *sits in his boxers. He plays with his balls.*

Mattie *inspects a circuit board.*

A bowl of cereal sits in front of her.

Mattie How big was it at least?

Clark I can't remember that far.

Mattie You just said –

Clark Not details though. Can't remember details, can I?

It was –

Big. It's a big thing.

She passes the board over.

Clazk (*inspecting*) You've seen em in books.

Mattie It's obviously not the same. It's a, a *visceral* –

Clark (*passing the board back*) No.

Mattie I feel like it's something you'd remember.

Clark My life's one big blur of sex and adventure, I can't be expected to remember every little thing that ever happened to me.

Mattie Where was it?

Clark South America someplace.

Mattie South America's gone.

Clark Not then it wasn't, was it. Not when I was six.

Mattie You were six.

Clark I was six and it was in this village down there. I was with my uncle.

Mattie And it was big.

Clark It was big.

Mattie And that's it.

Clark And . . . it was up on this truck.

So it was, you know, even bigger than that. Taller.

Mattie What about this.

She passes it over again.

Clark (*inspecting*)   . . . What am I looking at.

Mattie The transistor –

Clark No, it's fine. It's all fine. I told you.

He tosses it back to her.

Beat.

Mattie Why was it on a truck?

Clark Cos. They were taking it away.

Mattie Who was?

Clark They were – The blokes – Mexican . . .

Mattie Mexico's North America.

Clark Whatever they were. Mexican-looking lads. All stood round the truck with big guns, berets,

Mattie Why were *you* there?

Clark I said. I was visiting my uncle. He lived there and he was involved somehow. That's how I got close.

Mattie You're six and there's guns everywhere –

Clark My uncle *knows* the dudes with the guns. He's in*volved*.

He goes up to them while they're holding back the crowd –

Mattie What crowd?

Clark The crowd, there's a crowd. The whole place – All the little villager guys are trying to get to the truck, and the other guys are all waving guns at them like hallalahhallalahhallalah, Mexican or whatever –

Mattie Spanish.

Clark Spanish then –

Mattie Or not, Portuguese maybe.

Clark Some fucking thing – Hallalah, hallalah, get back, get back –

And they're all crying and shit,

Mattie So how did you –

Clark Because my uncle worked with em, like I said.

He talks to the main army guy in Mexican,

Mattie Spanish.

Clark Spanish –

Mattie Spanish or Portuguese.

Clark He talks to him like, baddababaddababaddababa, tells them to push the crowd back, let us through, give us some space. And they do, they all get shunted back and pushed away – And my uncle lifts me up and walks over and puts me up on the truck, and I touch it.

Pause.

Mattie And?

Clark What.

Mattie What was it like?

Pause.

Clark . . . Big.

Mattie Big.

Clark They're big. Big fucking tall things.

There's like the main pillar bit, in the middle, then all these webs and lines on top of it, and then the green bits. Leaves.

Mattie I know what they looked like –

Clark So there.

Mattie What was it *like* though. In, *experience* terms.

Pause.

Clark I dunno.

. . .

It's knobbly.

Main bit's all knobbly. Like rocks.

And the leaves . . .

They're like paper.

Old paper.

Like how paper used to be.

Mattie What did it smell like?

Clark It – I dunno.

You can't remember smells.

I looked at it, I touched it, I got the *gist*.

Then I got lifted back down, they lifted me back down again, and they drove it off.

All the villager guys all running after it shouting.

Chasing it down the road.

Pause.

Mattie That was wasted on you.

Clark Just a tree.

Mattie One of the last *ever*. Do you know how rare that was? To see it? To *touch* it?

Clark And cos I didn't stick my dick in it I'm a philistine.

Mattie You *are* a philistine.

People formed entire *religions* around the last trees.

Clark Yeah, mental people.

Mattie It's a big deal.

Clark Everything used to be a big deal. Coming out here would've been a big deal once.

Mattie It's not the same. My mum used to tell me stories about trees. *Fairy* stories.

Clark So?

Mattie So you touched something considered by an entire generation to be *mythic*. You literally touched the past. That's objectively a big deal.

Act One, II 17

And you're objectively a moron if you can't understand that.

Clark I'd say I'm objectively a legend.

Mattie It's our history.

Clark It's bullshit. History's bullshit. You're always asking everyone about it and it's *gone*. It doesn't exist. I don't waste my time thinking about shit that doesn't exist.

Mattie So you never think about the past then.

Clark No.

Mattie Not ever.

Clark No. That's why I'm way cooler than you.

Mattie What about the future.

Clark No. Same thing. Doesn't exist. Can't see it. Touch it. There's just this second, right now, as I'm saying it it's dying, it's gone. There it goes.

Pimps like me live in the present.

Cole *comes in to make his lunch.*

Clark You wanna talk to Cole about what a waste of fucking time worrying about tomorrow is.

Cole –

Cole tell us about your bomb shelter again.

Cole I'm busy.

Clark Just tell us though. Cole. Cole.

Mattie / I don't care –

Clark Tell us. Cole.

Mattie *gets up and leaves, taking her cereal with her.*

Enter **Gilda**.

Clark Cole.

Cole.

Gilda Clark –

Clark Cole tell Gilda about your bomb shelter.

Cole / I'm busy.

Gilda I don't care –

Clark Just tell us. Cole. Cole.

Tell us. Cole –

Cole I have a bomb shelter.

Clark Yeah, but –

Cole That's the story.

Clark Tell us about what it's all got though.

Gilda / I don't –

Cole Air filtration, water purifiers,

Clark All fucking kitted out, yeah –

Gilda / I've heard all this –

Cole It's a bomb shelter.

Clark And he got it cos he thought we were gonna get done –

Cole It seemed a strong possibility at the time.

Clark And how much was it?

Cole I already told you –

Clark Tell me again though –

Gilda Clark –

Cole I had to remortgage my apartment.

Clark WHAT A FUCKING RETARD!

He laughs hysterically.

Gilda Clark –

Clark His whole apartment!

Cole It was an investment.

Gilda Clark, can you –

Clark Why would you wanna stay around if everything's nuked to fuck anyway?

Gilda *Clark.*

Clark What?

Pause.

Gilda I asked you to clean that wall.

Clark What.

Gilda The wall. I asked you –

I asked you to clean it weeks ago –

Clark Days ago.

Gilda *Weeks* ago, I told you, I asked you to do it *weeks* ago –

Clark Nah it was like yesterday.

Gilda It doesn't matter when,

Clark Cole wasn't it just yesterday?

Gilda / It doesn't matter when it was –

Cole I don't –

Clark We're still running on Earth hours aren't we?

Gilda Don't start –

Clark Uni*versal* Time. Less you decided to switch us to a hundred and fifty-three hour days without letting us know?

Gilda All I've asked you to do –

Clark I don't think I'm allowed to.

Gilda Clark –

Clark My contract expired.

. . .

Right?

All our contracts expired. *Months* ago.

When they were meant to pick us up.

Cole *leaves with his lunch.*

Gilda The situation means –

Clark Supposed to be home by now.

I'm not insured.

I can't work if I'm not insured.

Gilda Everyone has to do their bit –

Clark That's not *my* bit. Cleaning isn't even *in* my contract.

I'm in a union –

Gilda We're all in a union –

Clark I can't be expected to do unpaid work –

Off-world unpaid work, which is often hazardous –

Gilda It's cleaning a wall.

Clark What if I go to do it and I slip and I fall down –

Gilda You're –

Clark Then I'm not just stranded on a cold dark rock in space, I'm stranded on a cold dark rock in space with a broken leg, or arm, or *spine*, with only very limited medical facilities –

Gilda Can you listen to me?

Clark You don't wanna get back to Earth and find a lawsuit waiting for you, that'd take the shine off the rescue, don't you think?

Gilda Can you *listen* to me for a second please?

Pause.

Gilda I only asked you –

Clark Why am I cleaning it off? You think I *want* to clean it off?

Gilda I'm just trying to –

Clark I'm not joking about the union –

Gilda Well *call them then*!

Pause.

Gilda Call them.

But to do that you'd have to actually do your *job* first and fix our communications –

Clark How many times do you want me to fucking tell you?

Comms are fine. They're *fine*.

Gilda Clearly they're not Clark, because if they were, we wouldn't still *be* here –

Clark I don't come into your little lab and start fucking around with your rocks, but you get to come and knock the dick out of *my* mouth whenever you want, and tell me what a shit job I'm doing when you don't know anything about it. *Anything*.

You think it's *my* fault we're still here.

You think it's *my* fault they haven't come to take us home –

Gilda That's not what I'm / saying –

Clark Every single transmission we've made has been marked as received.

. . .

Okay?

. . .

Do you get what that means?

. . .

Our computer. Their computers. Everything works.

Everything we send is getting to Earth.

Every broadcast. Video, audio, text. Received. Tick.

Everything's getting there.

Fine.

But no one's sending anything back.

. . .

No one's on *their* end of the phone.

. . .

Okay?

. . .

I can't make someone who's not *there* answer our transmissions.

Pause.

Gilda You're being ridiculous.

Clark Am I.

Gilda That's a completely – Ridiculous thing to assume –

Clark What is.

Gilda That they're – That everyone's just –

. . .

Pause.

Gilda We're all a bit –

Fraught.

From, from being out here so long,

not getting picked up when we're supposed to get picked up,

not having any contact for a few months –

Clark Six mon / ths.

Gilda *Nearly* six months.

Clark It's six –

Gilda Whatever it is, however long –

The last contact we had from them was delaying our return –

Clark By a few days –

Gilda So then maybe it got delayed more, there's a bigger delay and they can't get through to, to tell us when they're actually coming,

Clark They can get through fine.

Gilda We're billions of miles from Earth –

Clark So?

Gilda So *what's* more likely?

. . .

Sta*tistically*.

. . .

That the whole programme just decided to forget about us and leave us out here?

Or that in the space of six months the entire human race has dropped down dead?

. . .

. . .

Or is it possible, somewhere,

maybe,

in the *billions* of miles between here and there,

there's just maybe something *wrong*?

. . .

What do you think?

Mattie *has come back, listening in the doorway, unnoticed.*

Pause.

Clark Even if I did find something wrong,

I can't *do* anything with that information.

We can't go anywhere –

We can't get off the ground –

Gilda So what do you want me to say?

. . .

Tell me what I should say to you.

Pause.

Clark *picks up the circuit board.*

Pause.

Gilda Thank you.

. . .

And will you –

Clark I'll *clean* it.

Gilda Good. Thank you.

. . .

And maybe you could start wearing clothes again.

She leaves.

Pause.

Clark *grumbles something.*

Mattie What?

Beat.

Clark I said it won't make any difference.

In the transition, **Mattie** *leaves.*

Clark *puts some clothes on and cleans the X from the wall.*

It takes as long as it takes.

Act One, III 27

III.

Late.

Clark *and* **Ray**.

Ray Luscinia megarhynchos.

Clark Luscina –

Ray Luscinia.

Clark Luscinia –

Ray Luscinia megarhynchos.

Clark Luscinia mega –

Ray Megarhynchos.

Clark Luscinia megarhynchos.

Ray Nightingale.

Ray *blows a bird whistle.*

Clark That's nice. That's a nice one.

Ray Phylloscopus trochilos.

Clark Filla – I won't even – That's all yours, that one.

Ray Willow Warbler.

He blows a bird whistle.

Clark That's nice too.

Ray Regulus Regulus.

Clark Regulus Regulus. That's easier.

Ray Regulus Regulus, Goldcrest.

He blows a bird whistle.

Clark   Regulus Regulus.

. . .

I like the first one best.

Ray   Me too.

Clark   Luscinia –

Ray   Luscinia megarhynchos.

Clark   Nightingale. You can just say nightingale.

Ray   That's not the point though, is it.

He starts putting them away.

Clark   You blow em a lot.

Ray   Course I do.

Clark   A lot though, Ray. Arguably too much.

Ray   Do you know why?

Clark   Cos it's nice.

Ray   Course it's nice, goes without saying it's nice.

I wouldn't do it that much if it was just *nice*.

Clark   It's really nice.

Ray   I do it so I don't forget.

To *remember*.

Clark   Right.

Ray   Out here.

Clark   Yeah.

Ray No internet, no . . .

Clark You can't just listen to bird sounds.

Ray These are all I have.

And I have to blow em a certain way –

Clark To make the right sound.

Ray So if I don't blow em every day then they start to not sound right.

Then after a while I forget what they ever sounded like.

Then they're gone.

. . .

When you're away it's very easy to start forgetting.

Once you've detached yourself.

Clark But when you got back you could –

Ray Even then, even when I get back to Earth, there's only *recordings*.

And that's just another form of memory, cept it's a computer remembering instead of you.

. . .

I try very hard to hold onto birds in particular.

He blows a whistle.

Ray I'm just about old enough to remember the day they all fell out the trees.

. . .

My father comes in my room with a brush and says come help.

I follow him outside and they're all lying in the street.

Like stones wrapped in paper.

...

First the trees stopped singing. Then they stopped breathing.

The colour left.

Then the light.

Then nothing.

...

Beat.

Clark Fucking hell Ray.

Ray What.

Clark You're bringing me down.

Ray Well, you don't know. You've no memory of what it was like.

I'm the last generation that lived amongst the living.

Clark Let's play a game or something, Jesus.

He sets up Guess Who.

Ray Not this, let's play chess.

Clark You always beat me.

Ray That's why I like it.

Clark We're playing Guess Who. Pick a guy.

They look at the cards.

And don't just pick Bernard again, you always use him.

They pick cards.

Ray You're not interested in the past.

Clark Pimps live in the present, Ray.

Are you a guy or a girl?

Ray What? Oh. I'm a – Female.

Clark *flicks panels down.*

Ray They all think I'm an old fart too.

Clark I don't think you're an old fart Ray.

I just think you're depressing as fuck.

Ray That's what they all think.

Clark Who?

Ray On Earth. The pricks who write the cheques. Why do you think they sent me out here, with you lot? To a planet that's not a planet.

Clark I think it's alright.

Ray You've never been to Mars. Titan. Real planets.

Clark Titan's not a planet mate.

Ray More than this. More than rocks and ice and darkness.

Clark They reckon if we'd come here before the sun started fannying out it would've been almost daylight sometimes.

Ray Hmph.

Clark Ask me something.

Ray Are you male.

Clark Yes.

Ray *flicks panels down.*

Ray It's the biggest insult they could manage.

Making me ferry a bunch of green scientists out here then sit around waiting for someone half my age to come collect me.

We used to fly *back* from places too, not just ship these flat packs out.

Clark Someone's gotta set up base.

Do you have short hair.

Ray No.

Clark *flicks panels down.*

Ray There's a reason no one's been here before, it's that no one in their right mind would ever *want* to come here.

They know there's nothing useful here.

It's a financial work-around. It's a tax write-off.

This is where they send the new, the underqualified, the old.

And most of all the British. Mars is full of blonde Americans.

It's like they're building the master race out there.

He takes his pills.

Clark They should use you in the recruitment adverts Ray.

Ray Why did you want to do it?

Clark Do what?

Ray Come out here.

Clark I dunno . . .

Ray Are you wearing a hat?

Clark Wh – No.

***Ray** flips panels down.*

Ray There are reasons a person signs up to work this far from home.

Clark Gilda says she wanted to work off-world since she was a kid.

Ray Well she's a hopeless case. What about you. Why did *you* want to come out here.

Clark . . . Tax free's pretty good.

Ray It's a perk.

Clark You get to keep all your money.

Ray There are easier ways to avoid tax.

Clark I liked the idea. Being an astronaut.

Ray Yes.

Clark I liked all the old films.

Ray A symbol.

Clark Yeah –

Ray The last cowboys.

Clark And it's alright out here. I mean, the food's pretty bad –

Ray It's the same.

Clark Nah –

Ray It's just the same back there.

Clark A burger though –

Ray I remember when meat came from animals. Not a production line of Petri dishes.

Clark It tastes the same.

Ray How would you know?

Clark They say –

Ray Course *they* say, what are they likely to say it tastes like shit?

Clark Yeah, but –

Ray Who's going to prove them wrong, there's nothing left to kill to prove them wrong. Everything's dead.

Clark Tastes pretty good to me.

Ray Nothing tastes better than something that used to run around and have thoughts.

My mouth moistens up just thinking about it, and the last time I ate real meat I was five years old.

Just now, just thinking about it now.

It's moist city in here.

Clark That's great Ray.

Ray I don't even think about sex these days. Just food. *Real* food.

Clark *shakes his head.*

Ray You don't get that from the crap they feed us now.

It's like swallowing cardboard.

Clark It's not that bad.

Ray If those are your only reasons for being here . . .

Clark No, I like, I like all of it.

I get the annoying bits.

Staring at the same faces every day. No offence.

Recycled air, recycled water. Breathing each others' farts, drinking each others' piss.

And I've never gotten used to the bogs.

. . .

But I still like putting my suit on, when I'm checking the lines or whatever.

Going out on the surface.

Looking up at the moon, the stars.

Mist.

Everything.

It's class.

Ray Ever see anything else out there?

Beat.

Clark Like what?

Pause.

Clark Like –
Like what?

Pause.

Clark What else would I see out there?

Ray Are we playing this stupid game or what.

Pause.

Clark Uh – Do you have white hair.

Ray Yes.

Clark *flips panels down.*

Pause.

Ray Do you want to hear my secret plan?

Clark Are you Susan.

Ray Yes, well done, full marks. Do you want to hear.

Clark It's late, Ray.

Ray Late by whose watch? It's late in London but maybe it's lunchtime on Pluto.

Clark I don't live on Plutonian time.

Ray Do you want to hear.

Pause.

Clark What's your secret plan.

Pause.

Ray One of these runs, one time, maybe even this one, but one of them, wherever they send me, I'm not going back.

Pause.

Clark What – To Earth?

Ray Course to Earth, where else?

Clark You'd stay here.

Ray Here, there, wherever. One of these bases. They've got enough juice in these things for decades. Multiple missions. Indefinite timescale.

I could last it out comfortably.

Clark Why would you *want* to?

Ray Why would I want to go back? What have I got back there?

Two ex-wives and a bedsit full of old photographs.

That's not living.

Clark And out here is?

Ray There's nothing left back there. Trees. Birds. Animals. Countries gone.

Everyone crammed too close together on what's left of the land.

It's a shadow.

And they want to retire me. Trap me there.

Well fuck them.

I'll stay out here and go on my own terms.

Clark Ray, that's – Not a good idea.

Ray I'm not going to sputter out in my apartment where no one finds me.

Wait for the worms to eat me away. Stop being able to breathe through the smog.

Die in some riot I didn't even know was happening.

. . .

Everything that place was left a long time ago.

And I'd rather be dead a few billion miles away than alive in the wreckage.

IV.

Late.

Gilda *is alone.*

She eats from a box of cereal and looks out the window.

Her laptop's open on the table.

She walks the room, eating.

Mutters to herself.

There's a noise from above.

She stops.

Listens.

Someone's moving around up there.

We listen for a while.

Mattie *appears in the doorway, unnoticed.*

The sounds have stopped.

Gilda *squints to hear –*

Mattie   What / are you doing?

Gilda   Ah! Jesus –

You –

Made me jump.

Mattie *turns the lights on.*

Mattie   Why are you in the dark?

Gilda   Not completely dark –

Mattie   What were you doing, just then?

Gilda   I couldn't –

. . .

I thought you were up there, and I –

Mattie   I'm down here.

Gilda   I thought I heard someone.

Mattie   No one goes up there cept me.

Gilda   I know –

Mattie   You can't stand up in there.

Gilda   I just thought I heard someone.

. . .

Obviously I didn't.

Pause.

Mattie *goes to the ladder.*

Gilda   Don't –

Mattie Why?

Gilda It's – Stupid.

Mattie *goes up the ladder.*

Pause.

Mattie (*from above*) Oh my god . . .

Gilda What?

Mattie (*from above*) There's . . . Nothing up here.

Gilda Alright.

Mattie *comes back down.*

Gilda Don't need / to . . .

Mattie Everything that keeps us alive is up there, you probably heard the girls talking.

Gilda The girls?

Mattie The girls are what I call the oxygen and water systems.

Gilda Oh.

. . .

That's nice.

Mattie Are you eating cereal?

Gilda No, yes, just, Krispy Wows.

Mattie You eat them dry like that?

Gilda A bit. Sometimes.

Pause.

They stand there.

Mattie Well. Night.

She goes to leave.

Gilda Oh, Mattie –

I'd like to – To run tests on the, uh, 'girls' tomorrow. If that's okay.

Mattie I run tests every day.

Gilda I know –

Mattie That's my job.

Gilda I know, I'd just like to, watch.
If that's okay.

Mattie (*shrugs*) Whatever yanks your crank.

She goes to leave again.

Gilda I'd like to be more involved.

Mattie Okay.

Gilda I think it'd be useful.

Mattie You're the chief, Chief.

She goes to leave again.

Gilda Oh, sorry, Mattie?

I –

. . .

Why did you let me say Ray's name wrong?

. . .

Mattie His –

Gilda His surname.

. . .

. . .

I was saying it wrong. The whole time.

. . .

No one ever told me.

Pause.

Gilda And then at his, the funeral, the service thing we did, you were *laughing* –

Mattie It's not a big –

Gilda At his *funeral*.

Pause.

Mattie He thought it was funny. To not correct you.

It wasn't really about *you*, it was just . . .

Beat.

Gilda It's mean.

Mattie Yeah.

Gilda It's a mean thing to do to someone.

Mattie It is, yeah.

Gilda He might've liked me a bit more if I hadn't said his name wrong the entire time. *Years*.

Sih-bow-ski –

Mattie Suh-*botch*-ki –

Gilda I know *now* –

Mattie *nods.*

Gilda You told me after we'd wheeled him in the *freezer*.

Pause.

Did I do something to you at some point?

Mattie No –

Gilda Something I did that I didn't realise –

Mattie You didn't do anything –

Gilda Because I didn't *want* to be Captain –

Mattie I know –

Gilda And I'm well aware I'm terrible at it but I *have* to do it.

Mattie / You're n –

Gilda And you get to take the piss and not listen and have fun – don't you think *I'd* like to do that too?

Mattie / I –

Gilda You just leave me with Cole who is *no one* to talk to, *I* don't like him either but if I didn't talk to him I wouldn't talk to *anyone* –

And how am I supposed to be in charge if you both think I'm this total dickhead

Mattie / I don't –

Gilda who can't do anything right and doesn't get the jokes and makes you do work you don't want to do –

Well fuck me for trying to get us home, for trying to keep us together after everything that happened,

And –

And I can't *do* this, I can't *be* in charge or Acting Captain or whatever the paperwork says I have to be – I'm just / supposed to be studying *rocks*, I can't, I can't –

Mattie Please don't – Gilda –

Gilda.

. . .

. . .

I'm sorry.

. . .

. . .

Okay?

. . .

. . .

. . .

Are you crying?

Gilda No –

Mattie You're breathing weird –

Gilda   I'm – Fine.

Pause.

Mattie   . . . Is it cos you thought you heard a ghost?

Gilda   I didn't –

Mattie   Okay –

Gilda   I don't think I heard a ghost. It was just what you said.

Mattie   Right. The girls.

Gilda   The girls.

Mattie   Right.

Pause.

Gilda *gradually gets herself together.*

Gilda   That was unbelievably pathetic.

Mattie   No . . .

Gilda   Really, completely, pathetic.

Mattie   No, it was –

. . .

Fine.

. . .

. . .

Pause.

Mattie   I don't think you're a dickhead.

...

If you're . . .

. . .

And,

I don't think it matters if you're not good at being in charge.

Not that you're not good, I mean –

The wall's clean now, right?

You got that done.

Gilda You don't need to try and cheer me up.

Mattie I'm not – I'm just saying I don't think it's – I don't think it matters.

. . .

Because what even is there to be in charge *of* right now?

I mean –

We're just *waiting*. Waiting for someone to pick up the phone. Or come get us.

. . .

Or we're just waiting to die.

Gilda Don't say that.

Mattie Well it's true.

And there's nothing you can do about that.

We've got more than enough food. Water won't run out.

And the base is designed to last for *decades*, it'll still be breathing *way* after we've stopped. Its *job* is to live forever.

. . .

And that's the really scary thought.

. . .

I used to lie awake worrying about the windows cracking, now I worry about them *not* ever cracking.

. . .

You know?

. . .

Cos I would definitely punch my card if I thought I was just gonna be sat here.

Forever.

Staring at the walls.

Sat here till I lose every last one of my marbles and start eating my own shit without noticing the smell.

. . .

Gilda . . .

I said you didn't have to try and cheer me up.

Mattie I'm just saying I hope I go first.

Beat.

Gilda . . . Next.

. . .

You hope you go next.

Pause.

Mattie Right.

. . .

Yeah.

Pause.

Gilda *chews her hair.*

Mattie   What are you doing?

Gilda   Oh – (*Stopping.*)

Mattie   Do you do that a lot?

Gilda   Not –

Really.

Mattie   You were doing it just then.

Gilda   It's just when I'm anxious.

Mattie   I make you anxious?

Gilda   Everything makes me anxious. It's not you specifically.

Mattie   So you're always doing it.

Gilda   Not *always*.

Mattie   Why don't you just masturbate like everyone else?

Gilda   I don't – Does that help?

Mattie   Course it does. It's your release valve.

And what else are we meant to do all day anyway?

Gilda   I mean – Work –

Mattie   I'm on my DJ decks like three times a day.

Gilda   Three *times*?

Mattie   At least. I call it Nasturbating. Cos of Nasa.

Gilda   We're not with Nasa.

Mattie   I know, but, you know.

What about you?

Gilda I'm not –

Mattie Come on. We're talking.

Gilda I don't usually talk about –

Mattie Come *on* . . .

Beat.

Gilda I don't do a lot of DJ sets.

Mattie What, ever?

Gilda R –

Rarely.

Mattie You'd definitely feel way better about everything if you did.

Gilda I doubt it.

Mattie It's a good way of giving the day structure, too.

I know we're locked to Earth hours but it barely means anything when it's always dark, so if I rub one out morning noon and night it gives everything a bit more shape.

And it keeps me cool generally.

Gilda I just eat.

Mattie Yeah.

Gilda Or chew –

She chews her hair.

Mattie Well you definitely shouldn't do that.

Gilda I know.

Mattie Mostly because it makes you look touched but also because I read about this girl who died once and they didn't know why? So they opened her up and all her internal organs were like, *garrotted* with hair.

Gilda Right –

Mattie Because she chewed her hair.

Gilda Yeah, I mean, that's probably a myth.

Mattie I read it.

Gilda I'm not *swallowing* it –

Mattie No, but –

Gilda And if I did it'd go to my stomach, not my kidneys or my pancreas or wherever else.

Mattie Well maybe it's not a hundred per cent but the point remains it's not a good habit to have.

You're anxious though, you get anxious?

Gilda When I start thinking about never getting home.

Mattie Right, yeah, course. Sorry.

. . .

Who's waiting for you. Back there.

Gilda My –

. . .

Beat.

She frowns.

Mattie What?

Gilda Nothing, I –

. . .

I was about to say my mother.

Mattie Your mum's waiting for you?

Gilda No, she's –

Died.

Just before we left.

. . .

I don't know why I . . .

. . .

Beat.

Mattie Was she old?

Gilda Hm?

Mattie Your mum.

Gilda She was –

Quite old. Not so old.

She could've –

She was sick.

. . .

She got very . . .

Jumbled.

. . .

Mattie I'm sorry.

Gilda No, it's –

It's a long time ago now I guess.

. . .

Pause.

Mattie What are you listening to?

Gilda Oh – Nothing –

Mattie Come on, you never tell anyone what you're into.

Gilda It's nothing – I mean –

I don't sleep much at the moment, so it's just something to, um, relax to.

Mattie So what is it?

Gilda It's just –

. . .

With everything whirring away it never gets properly quiet in here, so I like to take a recorder out on surface walks and I, I'll record, you know, outside.

The nothing out there.

Beat.

Mattie You're listening to nothing.

Gilda And I sit here with the lights off and look out the window and sort of, zone out a bit.

Mattie Like meditation.

Gilda I guess. Almost. Kind of.

Mattie You can't just listen to a blank audio file?

Gilda It's different. It has a . . .

An organic quality. The type of silence I get.

It – Breathes.

Mattie It doesn't.

Gilda No, I know, but – It's – Real. Real . . . nothingness.

Beat.

Mattie I only asked to change the subject but this is more depressing.

Gilda (*laughs*) It's not, I like it.

It's nice.

Pause.

Mattie Do you want to hear a story about Ray?

Gilda About Ray?

Mattie It's kind of amazing.

Gilda It's not another attempt to cheer me up.

Mattie No –

Gilda I don't want to hear some . . . I don't want to make fun –

Mattie It's not –

Gilda Some mean story about –

Mattie It's not, I promise.

Pause.

Mattie Okay?

Gilda Okay.

Mattie Okay –

So –

This is,

I don't know,

a while ago.

Maybe a few weeks before he died.

And I'm in here and he's in here and it's late, he always liked to sit up late.

I don't think he slept much.

And he was in a weird mood, I don't know,

Maybe he'd been drinking but he didn't *seem* –

He just seemed tired. Stressed, or whatever.

And we talk for a bit even though he's kind of distracted and cagey and just being generally –

Weird.

And that was one of the days I'd been outside to check all the lines, and he started asking me, Did I see anything out there, Did I see anything out there.

And I thought –

I was saying –

In the sky? The mist? Shooting stars?

And he says no, Did I *see* anything.

Gilda See what?

Mattie This is what I'm asking, I'm like, Like what? What else would I see out there?

And he says 'I saw something'.

. . .

And I say what, because he barely even went outside, what could he see just sitting here, but he says —

'I saw a girl.'

. . .

. . .

He says 'I saw a girl. At the window.'

. . .

. . .

So I thought he was joking, or, I mean, sometimes he said pretty weird things,

so I didn't —

But he's just staring at me, completely like —

Like slate.

. . .

. . .

He says I saw a little girl.

Maybe four or five. Small.

Looking in at him. Watching.

. . .

. . .

And after a while she just walks away, out of sight.

And he goes looking out all the windows all over trying to, to see where she went to, but he can't see her.

She's gone.

. . .

. . .

...

Isn't that amazing?

Gilda A girl –

Mattie Just stood outside the window. Watching him.

Pause.

Gilda But –

Mattie I mean, obviously it's impossible but that's not the point.

The point is he really *believed* he saw it.

I believed, that he believed.

And after that, for the last month he was –

Well.

...

And now he's gone.

Pause.

Mattie I just thought, since you thought *you* heard something –

Gilda I didn't –

Mattie I know, but –

You know.

Pause.

Gilda That's awful.

Mattie   I know.

Gilda   It's –

Mattie   I know.

Pause.

Gilda   Poor Ray.

Mattie   Poor Ray.

Pause.

Mattie   Oh man,

I even missed the –

He said she had a,

The girl?

She had a kind of a –

The mouth.

It was all fucked up.

Beat.

Gilda   What do you mean.

Mattie   Instead of a mouth she had this –

Scar.

A big scar or a scab or something.

Gilda   Like what?

Mattie   Like this –

She slowly draws an X across her mouth with her finger.

Pause.

He kept saying – What happens when she gets inside?
What happens when she gets in here?

. . .

. . .

'What happens when she gets inside?'

Pause.

Mattie Can I hear some of your silence?

Gilda Oh –

It won't really work out the speakers –

Mattie *puts the headphones on and hits play.*

She stands and listens to the silence.

Mattie It's nice . . .

Pause.

Mattie *takes the headphones off and puts them on* **Gilda**.

Mattie Night.

She leaves.

Pause.

Gilda *tries to relax.*

A crackle.

A voice starts to pull out of the laptop.

Then fills the theatre.

Voice Hellooooo . . .

. . .

Hello!

Laughter.

The voice of a very young girl.

Gilda *tries to locate the source- She checks her laptop, closes it.*
The voice remains.

Ah-Boo!

Ah-Boo!

Boo!

BOO!

. . .

onetwothreefourfivesixseveneightblargleblargleblurrblurr
blrrfff –

Laughter.

I was just in there . . . I was– and– I was in there–

. . .

Well you have to– If you don't then you have to– Because you didn't–

Brrrrrrush brush brush

. . .

And all the people you said to–

The lights drop, leaving us alone with the voice.

It whispers–

All the, the colours.

. . .

and if you, if you don't, then you can, you can put it with the, for when you can have it for when you're–

For when you *need* it.

So you can always have them . . .

. . .

with the skyyyyy . . . . . .

Laughter.

V.

Late.

Cole *is working at the table with paper and pencil.*
Clark *is semi-clothed, tossing a ball around.*

He starts hurling the ball against walls and catching it.
He hums and sings tunelessly. Big sighs and annoying noises.

This goes on for a while.
Cole *is visibly irritated.*

Eventually **Clark**'s *ball crashes into the kitchen unit, clattering plates everywhere.*

Cole Can you do that somewhere else.

Clark I'm *bored* man. So *bored*.

Cole Be bored somewhere else.

Clark Usually when I'm bored I'll have a wank but I've used up all my porn.

He bounces the ball again.

I never thought that'd happen. I brought *so* much.
But we've been here so long now.

. . .

I wish I'd brought more normal films to be honest.

. . .

What films have you got?

...

Can I copy some of your films?

...

Cole.

...

Cole.

...

Cole.

...

Cole –

Cole I don't have any.

Clark What?

Cole I don't like films.

Beat.

Clark What do you mean? Who doesn't like *films*?

Cole I don't like anything fictional.

Clark Why?

Cole Because it's made up. I don't like things that aren't real.

Pause.

Clark You're a fucking weirdo man. That is such a weird thing to say.

What kind of reason is that?

What are you doing anyway?

He picks up some of **Cole**'s *papers.*

Cole Don't touch that –

Clark Maths? You do know maths is for benders, yeah?

Cole Put it down.

Clark This is what you do instead of watching films. Recreational maths.

He goes back to throwing his ball.

Cole I'm trying to work –

Clark Do you think I'm mean to Gilda?

Cole I don't know –

Clark I don't mean to be –

Like I mean I do,

But it gets out of hand.

And I like her too, I think she's alright.

She just gets well stressed. About us being stuck here so long.

And I am too you know, I just don't see what we can do about it.

So I don't worry about it.

. . .

But you never seem bothered about anything.

You're always just the same.

But I bet it's hardest for you, actually.

Cole Why.

Clark Cos you've got a kid.

Cole Oh. Yes.

Clark I don't think I'd even *come* out here if I had a kid. If I had a kid I'd want to be there. For *every*thing.

...

Do you miss him loads?

...

Do you reckon he's in your bomb shelter now?

...

How old is he?

...

Cole.

...

Cole.

...

Cole –

Cole What can I say that'll make you go somewhere else.

Clark Why can't you go somewhere else?

Cole I – Need something in here.

Clark You need a calculator mate, your maths is gash.

Beat.

Clark Do you miss Ray?

Cole What do you mean.

Clark I think about him a lot. I sometimes –

Cole What do you mean about my maths.

Beat.

Clark It's ballbags. It's wrong.

Cole How would you know.

Clark Because I'm a Mathematician and Computer Scientist, dickhead.

Fuck's sake, everyone thinks I'm a total retard round here –

Cole You only saw it for a second.

Clark Long enough to smell the shit in your equations.

Do you want me to write you an algorithm?

Beat.

Cole What for?

Clark (*makes a face*) Ummnnh! To help solve whatever you're trying to solve quicker.

Beat.

Cole How long will that take.

Clark Depends.

Cole On what.

Clark On whether I want to do it or not.

Beat.

Cole I can do it myself.

Clark Alright then.

He throws his ball at the walls again.

Pause.

Cole What do you – What do you want.

Clark For what.

Cole For the algorithm.

Clark I don't want anything mate. Just respect. Brotherhood.

And that laser pointer keyring you have, I want that.

Cole My keyring.

Clark It's a big job, writing an algorithm.

Beat.

Cole *sighs and takes his keys out.*

He works the laser pointer off the ring and passes it to **Clark**.

Clark Nice.

Cole Now – Stop that –

Clark *is shining it in* **Cole**'s *face.*

Cole Stop it. Write it for me.

Clark What's it for.

Cole I gave you the keyring –

Clark I can't write it without details, can I?

What's it for, what are we looking for?

The un*known*.

What's X?

Pause.

What?

Cole I can give you the figures, but –

Clark S'alright, not that bothered. This got old anyway –

He tosses the keyring and goes to leave.

Cole Time. X is time.

Pause.

Clark Time.

Cole *nods*.

Clark You want an algorithm for time.

Pause.

There's a clock right there mate.

You're taking the long way round.

And we're wearing watches –

Cole Watch it. Watch.

They watch the clock.

Time passes.

Clark What are you –
Cole Watch.

Pause.

The display stutters, faults,

then snaps backwards one hour and forty-three minutes.

Pause.

Clark What – What was that.

Pause.

It's broke. Why didn't you tell me, now I have to –
Cole You can't fix it.
Clark (*checking watch*) What time do you –
Cole You can't fix it.

. . .

The watches are the same. The computers.

They're all the same.

...

Everything's linked to Earth through the main clock.

And the main clock's wrong.

Pause.

Clark How long's it been like that?

Cole I don't know.

Clark But you're –

Cole How could I tell?

...

It goes back every night. Multiple times.

Sometimes in the day too, but not as often.

...

And that's what we're assuming's day and night.

Clark Every day.

Cole Sometimes minutes, sometimes hours. Sometimes it just slows down.

...

It's been doing it more recently. That's why we've been sleeping so badly.

Pause.

Clark We don't know what time it is.

Cole No.

Clark Or what day.

Cole No.

Pause.

Clark So we don't know long we've been here.

Cole No.

Clark We think it's nearly three years –

Cole It's more. Maybe lots more.

We had a day 'last week' that lasted at least fifty hours.

You had a lot of naps.

Pause.

Clark But we're – No – It's not –

Cole Will you do the algorithm now.

Clark Why didn't we notice?

Cole A day here is six and a half Earth days.

And the sun's barely visible and we're always inside.

It's one long night.

That's why they fixed everything to Universal Time on Earth.

It's supposed to be more reliable.

Clark   But it's *fucked*.

Cole   Yes.

The computers don't log Plutonian time either.

Which is why I need the algorithm.

Clark   That wouldn't –

If it's that random there's no way you could ever –

Cole   I know. It's more of a hobby.

Beat.

Clark   What about – What did Gilda say?

Cole   What.

Clark   When you told her.

Cole   I didn't tell her.

Clark   Why?

Cole   Why would I.

Clark   She's in charge –

Cole   She can't do anything. No one can do anything.

The fault's somewhere between here and Earth.

Clark   That's not the point –

Cole   What would it achieve.

Clark   If you'd told someone as soon as you'd –

Cole   I don't know how long it was doing this before I noticed.

Or even how long since I noticed.

It would have made no difference.

Clark You told me.

Cole You made me tell you.

Clark So you've just been watching us like lab rats?

Cole I didn't think you'd want to know.

Do you feel better knowing.

Pause.

Clark No.

Pause.

This is why a lot of the systems keep glitching.

Cole Everything's centralised.

Beat.

Clark Well what can we – There's gotta be –

He rifles through **Cole**'s *notes and finds an analogue watch.*

Cole It's broken. I think he wore it just because.

Clark He –

. . .

How did you get this?

. . .

Did you take this off his body?

Pause.

Cole I needed –

Clark The fuck is *wrong* with you?!

Cole It wasn't –

Clark You took this off his *wrist* –

Cole It was *important*. There's no time to be sentimental when we're –

Clark He was our friend –

Cole He wasn't my friend.

Clark Well he was still a human being for *fuck's* sake.

. . .

He pockets the watch.

Pause.

Cole There's no point getting upset.

. . .

Can't get it back now.

Clark *looks up at the clock.*

Pause.

I don't know how old I am.

The clock faults again –

VI.

Late.

The table is strewn with photographs.

Ray *sits clutching a bloody cloth to his arm.*

Gilda *looks on.*

Pause.

Ray Even if we were in contact with them, what would they do.

Pause.

Gilda That's not the point.

Ray I doubt they'd care enough to spend a few million sending a taxi home for me.

Gilda Ray –

Ray They'd just tell you to restrain me. Keep me tied up for months till whichever young prick they send shows up. If he does ever show up.

Gilda You're not allowed to downplay this.

Pause.

Ray Don't tell the others.

Gilda I have to –

Ray You don't have to do anything, and there's nothing *to* downplay because it's nothing, it's nothing to make a fuss about –

Gilda I have to / take some kind of action –

Ray No, no, no, no, Don't tell Clarky. Clark. Don't tell him.

Pause.

Ray Alright?

Gilda I –

Ray Don't –

Gilda *Okay.*

. . .

It's not as if they could – We can't *take* you anywhere, can we.

Beat.

Ray Embarrassing enough.

. . .

Looking at me the way you did . . .

Gilda I helped you.

Ray I don't need you to pity me.

Gilda Keep your voice down, one of them could walk in any minute.

If that's what you're scared of.

Ray I don't need your pity.

Gilda Okay. You don't have it.

Pause.

You have a real –

Ray What.

Gilda . . .

You have a real issue with women.

Beat.

Ray Where do you get that from?

She makes a face.

Ray I may have an issue with *you* –

Gilda And what have I ever done to you?

Ray The whole *planet* has an issue with women –

Gilda Which planet would that be.

Ray I'm not prejudiced.

I'm an *astronaut*.

Gilda The two aren't mutually – You're dripping on your photos –

She moves the photos away from the pooling blood.

Ray Don't touch those –

Gilda You're covering them in blood.

She moves them to safety then starts to change his cloth for a clean one.

Pause.

Ray You didn't cry.

Gilda Did you expect me to.

Ray You cry a lot.

Gilda This wasn't such a surprise. With your behaviour recently.

Ray . . .

Pause.

Gilda How will you explain the blood.

Ray I'll clean it.

Gilda What about the cut.

Ray I won't wear short sleeves.

She dabs blood from the photos.

Ray Be careful with those, they're extremely old.

Gilda I am – I know – It's your blood.

Pause.

Are these relatives? Ancestors?

Ray I don't know any of these people.

Gilda You have pictures of strangers.

Ray I collect them.

Gilda You collect old photographs.

Ray That's very valuable that one –

Gilda Al*right*.

Ray ... It was taken on an early space flight. Nineteen sixties.

...

Damn near bankrupted myself getting hold of that one.

Gilda You can't just look at them online?

Ray They exist.

No one has anything that *exists* anymore.

Everything you own is just ones and zeroes.

...

They have a life.

Light trapped in paper.

Something from then I can hold onto now.

He looks at the photo.

Ray Back when space travel meant something.

When people cared.

Gilda Some people still care.

Ray *No one* cares.

They care so much they've ditched us here and cut off contact.

Gilda It's a technical fault, they'll fix it.

Ray And how are you on your history, because we didn't send anyone anywhere for *decades* –

Gilda We've always launched –

Ray Not people.

Not people.

The only reason we even *started* way back when was just to fuck Russia.

Beat them to the first rock in spitting distance.

Once we started having our wars with countries that used *sticks* for weapons there was no threat of any of *them* getting out to Mars. Europa.

Gilda We have people on both now.

Ray Just your lot.

Scientists. People looking at rocks.

And only since the birds dropped out the trees.

Only to find some way of prolonging whatever paltry existence we can manage on our own planet. The one we *ruined*. It's too *late*.

Gilda Ray, this isn't –

Ray All that'll happen next is the rich'll start shipping themselves out to their own private tin cans like this one, on whichever planet they can afford.

And no one gives a damn. Earth is pissing its last and everyone's just looking at their fucking shoes.

Gilda Ray –

Ray When I get back they're going to *retire* me, do you understand? They don't give two shits about an old cunt like me –

Gilda *Ray.*

Ray *catches his breath.*

Pause.

Gilda If this is what you're worried about I'd have thought you'd be happy with the current situation. Happy enough not to –

Ray Is anyone waiting for you. Back there.

Beat.

Gilda No.

Ray Me either.

. . .

Last run I did I thought about messing with the comms.

Pause.

Gilda Did you – Are you the reason –

Ray No.

Gilda Did you do something to the –

Ray *No.*

. . .

I said I thought about it, I'm not. . .

. . .

. . .

I'm not like that.

Pause.

Gilda Okay.

Pause.

Ray I used to want to stay out here but the thought of that now, with everything. . .

. . .

Rotting away inside these walls.

. . .

Watching it all stretch out in front of me.

. . .

Can't go back, can't stay here. . .

Gilda You can go back. We're all going back.

Someone will come and get us.

. . .

But I need to know if I need to watch you.

Ray Hide the knives.

Gilda I'm serious. Is this a real attempt, or,

. . .

Do we need to have you on watch?

He looks out the window.

Gilda Ray.

Pause.

Ray.

VII.

Late.

The room is dark, few lights on.

Ray *sits alone, finishing tearing the last of his photographs into pieces.*

He's weeping.

His hand stifles much of the sound as his body wracks with sobs.

We watch him for a while.

Eventually he calms.
Catches his breath.

He looks exhausted.

A fluttering.

A whistle,
A fluttering.

Ray *looks up –*

A fluttering.

There's a bird in here.
It whistles.
Luscinia megarhynchos.

Ray *stands and tries to get near it.*

It flutters about the ceiling, looping, circling.

Ray　Hello . . . hello pretty one . . .

He drags a chair closer and stands on it, the bird just out of reach.

Ray　Come on now, come and, don't be shy, come and –

With a whistle the bird swoops up through the access hatch into the space above.

Wait, waitwaitwait . . .

He clambers up the ladder and disappears after it.

We hear fainter whistling, fluttering from above.

Ray (*from above*) Don't be scared – Don't – Come here with me, come with me –

One of the cupboard doors in the kitchen opens.

The clock glitches and scrambles a little.

More whistling.

Ray (*from above*) There we are, I got you, I got you, don't worry –

Ray *climbs back down the ladder, clutching his hands together carefully –*

Ray I got you, I got you.

Don't worry, shhhhhshshshshsh –

What a pretty one you are, what a pretty one, eh?

. . .

Let's have a look at you, let's have a little –

He opens his hands very gently but finds them empty.

There's a rustling coming from the open cupboard.

Ray *turns to see.*

The clock begins to glitch and scramble more.

A **Girl** *is crawling out into the room backwards.*

Maybe four or five years old.

Ray stares as she emerges.

She stands and turns to face him.

Where her mouth should be, a large X is carved into her face.

She watches **Ray**.

He takes a penknife from his pocket and flicks it open.

He stabs it brutally into his neck, over and over and over.

He hacks at the tendons, windpipe, jugular.

Blood cascades down his front in rivers and waves.

He drops the knife and grabs at the gore spilling from his neck.

He turns to the wall and stumbles against it, gurgling, choking, yelping.

88 X

He paints a vast, smeared X onto the wall with the colour that pours from him.

Hands slap and drag against the wall.

The clock is frozen on unreadable characters.

The **Girl** *watches.*

Black.

A_ct Two

I.

The same.

The room is messier. More cluttered and dirty.

The clock above the window is frozen on glitched characters.

Gilda *and* **Mattie** *are slumped on the floor.*

Mattie *wears a space suit.*

She vomits into the helmet she cradles between her legs.

Pause.

She spits.

Gilda   Do you want –

Something else.

. . .

To do that in.

Mattie *spits.*

Mattie   I've half-filled it now.

Might as well keep going.

She spits.

Mattie   Does it smell?

Gilda   . . . what?

Mattie *spits.*

Pause.

Mattie   You didn't want to let me in.
Gilda   I thought you were –
Mattie   I scared you. At the window.

Pause.

She spits.

It was a long time.
Gilda   We thought everyone had . . .

I stopped believing anyone was coming.

Pause.

Everything stopped working . . .

Pause.

Mattie   The girls –
Gilda   They're still . . .
But everything . . .

We lost all the –

All our computers.

. . .

Everything we had left.

From Earth.

. . .

Everything went.

Beat.

We can't – We don't –

She gestures to the clock.

It stopped.

. . .

Everything stopped.

. . .

. . .

I don't know what it even. . .

Pause.

Mattie   So you don't know how long –
Gilda   Tell me again.

Mattie ...

Gilda Tell me – Start again –

...

They *sent* you here.

Pause.

Mattie I'm here.

Gilda You're here to take us home.

...

Tell me again.

Mattie I'm here.

Gilda Can I touch you?

...

Just to –

...

...

To be sure?

Pause.

They reach out across the gap.

They touch.

[ ]

The same.

Gilda, **Cole**, *and* **Clark**.

Gilda *chews her hair.*

Pause.

Cole Start again.

Clark I don't get it.

Pause.

Clark I don't get what you mean.

Cole Start again.

Gilda I told you –

Cole Tell it again. Tell us. Start again.

Pause.

Cole You're in here.

Pause.

Cole Start a / *gain* –

Gilda Al*right*.

. . .

I'm in here. It's,

I'm sitting –

Cole Where.

Gilda Just – Here.

Cole And you see –

Gilda Don't *prompt* me.

I see her.

Cole At the window.

Gilda At the window –

Clark What's she look like?

Gilda Like a – Person.

Cole Like what.

Gilda Like a person looks.

Small –

Clark Is she smiling?

Gilda I can't – I can't see her face because of the – The reflection.

Cole Then she disappears.

Gilda She doesn't disappear, she goes, she goes around to the airlock –

Cole She comes in –

Clark You let her in?

Gilda No, I – She –

Cole She gets in here. She gets inside.

Clark How come you're in here then?

Gilda Because I, I back away –

Clark You're scared.

Gilda She hasn't taken the helmet off and I back away and I fall,

Cole And you're in here.

Gilda And she takes her helmet off and sits and, she's, ah, sick. Into the helmet.

Beat.

Clark What?

Cole Why.

Gilda Because she just landed, she's nauseous, she doesn't feel / well, she –

Clark She's travel / sick.

Gilda No –

Cole Does it smell.

Gilda What?

Cole Can you smell it.

Gilda Why / would I –

Clark What's that / matter?

Cole *Can you smell the vomit.*

Gilda I don't –

No.

I don't know.

You can't remember smells.

Beat.

Clark It's a weird thing to ask.

Cole Then what.

Gilda We're talking. I'm not – I don't say much.

Cole Why.

Gilda Because I'm, In shock. I'm just trying to listen, she asks me questions, but I can't get much out, I'm –

Cole What questions.

Gilda Where everyone is –

Cole Where we are.

Clark Does she know our names?

Gilda No. Yes. Probably. I guess she does but doesn't say –

Clark How does she know?

Gilda Because they *sent* her here.

. . .

Cole What else.

Gilda She – She says it's the middle of the day.

Clark What?

Gilda She asks where you are and I tell her you're asleep and she says it's the middle of the day. It's strange you're asleep because it's the middle of the day by, by Universal – By their time.

Beat.

Gilda So I show her the clock and she asks how long it's been like that and I say we can't tell and she says we've been out of contact a long time,

Cole How long.

Gilda She didn't say –

Cole You didn't *ask* her –

Gilda *No.*

I didn't.

. . .

Alright?

Pause.

Gilda She asks about Ray.

Clark About Ray?

Gilda She asks to see the captain and I tell her.

Clark What does she / say?

Cole Does she ask to see the body.

Gilda No.

Clark Why would she want to?

Cole To prove she's not lying.

Clark Why would she lie?

Gilda She didn't ask.

. . .

I just told her.

Beat.

Cole Then what else.

Gilda Then nothing.

Then you come in and you see her and you ask all the same questions.

Cole And *what* do we ask.

Gilda You were th / ere –

Cole Tell me. You tell me what I asked.

Pause.

Gilda . . .

You ask her about Earth. You ask her –

You don't ask her name –

You're rude to her.

You're suspicious.

Cole She *is* suspicious.

Gilda She's here to take us home.

Cole Why do they send one person. Why is she alone.

Gilda She tells you.

Cole It doesn't make sense.

Gilda It's expensive.

Clark They need room in the shuttle to take us home.

Gilda You don't ask her how long it's been. What the date is.

Cole She doesn't *tell* us –

Gilda She just wants to eat.

Cole And what does she eat.

Gilda / Cereal.

Clark Krispy Wows.

Cole All she wants after six months of travel is cereal.

Clark What does that matter?

Gilda She can eat on her ship.

Clark That's what you're worried about?

Cole What are we talking about.

Gilda She wasn't starving –

Cole What are we *talking* about.

Gilda Earth.

Cole *Specifics*.

Clark Calm down / man –

Gilda *Trees*.

. . .

. . .

She tells us her tree story.

Pause.

Cole What tree story.

Clark I don't remember that.

Pause.

Gilda She tells us she saw one.

She was with one of the last trees.

When it was dying.

. . .

It's up on the back of a, a truck in this village somewhere, and she's lifted up to touch it, and there's all these men with guns –

Clark That's my story.

Pause.

Gilda What?

Clark That's my story, I told you that.

Pause.

Gilda No, no –

Clark In South America.

Gilda Yes, and the military are all –

Clark This is my story, this happened to me.

Gilda No –

Clark I was six. My uncle lifted me through the crowd. Onto the truck. I touched it.

I told you this.

Gilda ...

She –

Clark I told you this ages ago, you always wanted to hear hippy stuff like that.

Pause.

Cole Why would she tell you this. The trees died decades before we got here.

It's not news.

Beat.

Clark I was six.

Pause.

Gilda ...

Stop looking at me like that –

Cole What's wrong with you.

Gilda Nothing's *wrong* with me –

Cole Then why –

Gilda Maybe I'm just confused because, she was,

she was talking about Earth, and you were talking about Earth,

It's not –

It's not indicative of anything like you're –

...

Stop *staring* at me.

...

...

You're asking me all these questions and they're all,

And it's not –

It doesn't *mean* anything.

...

...

...

Yes, okay, maybe I do remember you told me,

I just got it –

I got muddled with the,

or maybe I heard it from the girl who used to manage life systems,

maybe you told her and she told me and that's how I, I –

It doesn't matter, what matters is –

Clark What girl.

Gilda Fuck *off*.

Cole *He* manages life systems. He's tech. *What* girl.

Pause.

Gilda This must have been a different, another –

Cole You said it was your first time out here.

Gilda I know –

Cole You never worked off-world before.

Gilda I *know*.

Cole So then *what*.

Pause.

Cole What are you *saying*.

Gilda We had a –

...

...

I –

. . .

. . .

She was *here*. We talked a lot. She liked to hear about the past –

She was the one Ray told about the, the things he was seeing, she told me about Ray's –

Clark   I told you that.

Gilda   Stop it!

Clark   Ray told *me* about the girl at the window, *I* told you, *I* told you that.

Pause.

Gilda   . . .

Cole   She's gone.

Gilda   I'm not –

Cole   She's lost it.

Gilda   Don't *fucking* talk about me like I'm not here – I'm *here*, / I'm –

Cole   The last person who started seeing girls who weren't there opened his throat on the walls.

Clark   Leave her alone, it doesn't mean she's –

Gilda   I don't need you to defend me, I am not – I can – Whatever you're –

Cole   How many people on our crew.

Gilda   What?

Cole   Including Ray. How many.

Gilda Four.

Cole Four. One, two, three, and one in the freezer. Where's this extra girl.

Pause.

Cole One two three, one in the freezer.

Where's the fifth.

Where's this extra person.

Who *is* this person.

Gilda . . . she was –

Cole *What.*

Gilda How do I know that it's not –

That *you* both forgot, or, or that you're both just *saying* this to, / to –

Clark I wouldn't do that to / you . . .

Cole You're talking with *ghosts.*

Gilda I'm not – I don't – And if I am then so are you, you *both* talked to her –

Cole Who. Which one. There's two now, which one did we talk to?

Gilda The *one* – The one from *Earth*. They sent her to take us home, you *saw* her.

Talked to her. You *said* –

Cole So where *is she*.

Gilda She said, you saw, I told you, she went out on the surface, / she's outside, she –

Clark Let's maybe, we / should maybe chill our boots here –

Cole You told us –

Gilda This morning –

Cole How do you know when morning was?

Clark / I don't think this is a good –

Gilda She's *here*.

Cole Where? And how did she *get* here.

Gilda A ship, a shuttle, a, a,

Cole Have you seen it.

Gilda . . .

Cole Did you see what she supposedly arrived in.

Beat.

They both rush to the window and scan the surface.

Clark Let's just all take a / sec and –

Cole *Where*.

Gilda Check the – It'll be on the other side –

They hurry off, **Cole** *orders* **Clark** –

Cole Check that side, you check that side –

They split.

Pause.

They come back on. **Cole** *limps heavily from now on.*

Gilda No?

Clark (*shakes head*) No.

Gilda *rushes to check* **Clark***'s side.*

Clark Maybe we can't see though, it's further away –

Cole There's nothing there.

Gilda *comes back.*

Clark She left already –

Cole We didn't notice?

Clark We were sleeping,

Gilda It'll be out there somewhere, we just –

Cole It never happened. She was never here.

Beat.

Gilda You *saw* her.

Cole There's no one here. It's a mirage.

Gilda You can't *touch* a mirage –

Mirages don't talk.

Mirages don't eat *cereal* –

They *sent* someone.

. . .

. . .

You saw her, didn't you.

You saw her.

Beat.

Clark   ... I mean ... I think I did ...

Cole   You didn't see anything.

Clark   I can – Sort of – *Feel* it. I feel like I saw someone.

Cole   She's telling you your own stories.

Gilda   That wasn't –

Cole   She told us some fiction and enough time's passed that she's convinced us it's fact.

Gilda   That's ludicrous –

Cole   She's implanted a false memory, / she drilled us –

Gilda   How would I – That's impossible –

Cole   She's convinced us that something that never happened happened.

Gilda   Why would I do that?

Cole   Because you're *insane*.

...

...

Do you even think this is the first time we've had this argument?

Pause.

Gilda   You *saw* her ...

...

You said, you both said, you both – You *talked* to her –

Cole Don't talk to me anymore.

Gilda You don't get to *diagnose* me –

Cole The more she says the more at risk we are –

Gilda If I am what you're – Then so are you, so are *both* of you, I'm not making up people who aren't *there* –

Cole Stop talking –

Gilda Whatever's happening is happening to you too, it's –

Cole Shut *up* –

He grabs at her throat and face, forcing her to the floor –

Cole / Shut *up*, shut your *mouth* –

Clark Hey –!

Gilda / Get *off* me –

Cole Help me with her, *help* me with her –

Clark *wrestles* **Cole** *away –* **Gilda** *manages to squirm out of his grip.*

Clark What's *wrong* with you?

Cole She is *dangerous*, she is *delusional* –

Clark You're acting like a fucking maniac –

Cole This has to be fixed *now*. She is putting our sanity at risk which is putting our *lives* at risk. She is dragging us into her own psychotic world, and I will not let her jeopardise our entire perception of what's –

My *daughter* is waiting for me.

Gilda Son, you have a son Cole –

Cole *Whatever she is*, I don't have to –

. . .

What is this –

Why am I –

. . .

. . .

Why am I walking like this?

Pause.

Cole What's wrong with me.

Gilda *and* **Clark** *look to each other.*

Cole What.

. . .

What have you *done* to me.

Gilda No one's done anything to you –

Clark You forgot again.

Gilda Clark –

Cole Forgot what.

. . .

Forgot *what*.

Beat.

Clark You always tell him better than I do –

Cole Tell me *what*.

...

What are you –

Gilda It's cancer.

Pause.

You have can / cer –

Cole You shut your *cunt* mouth Gilda, you, *you* tell me –

...

You tell me what this is, I don't trust her, I don't –

You tell me.

Beat.

Clark We keep telling you –

Cole You never told me anything –

Clark You keep forgetting.

...

We tell you then you, you forget again.

...

I'm sorry.

Cole ...

...

You don't,

You don't *forget* something like that.

. . .

How do you *forget* that you –

That you're. . .

. . .

You're lying to me, you're with her, you're both, you're trying to make me believe that I'm –

Gilda Why are you walking like that?

Beat.

Cole . . . what.

Clark What's with your leg?

Gilda Why are you limping.

Cole I'm . . .

Clark You sleep on it weird?

Cole It's nothing –

. . .

There's nothing wrong with me –

Gilda It's probably nothing.

Clark Let her scan it so you can shut up about it –

Cole No –

Gilda It's a tumour.

Cole Stop it –

Gilda I'm sorry.

Clark You forgot again –

Cole Stop doing this – Stop it –

Gilda I'm sorry. Do you remember?

Clark We scanned you mate, remember?

Cole What have you done to me –

Gilda No one's done anything to you –

Clark You forgot again.

Gilda You keep forgetting –

Cole You shut your *cunt* mouth Gilda, you, you tell me –

Clark You always tell him better than I do –

Cole *You* tell me.

Gilda You have a tumour.

Clark It's cancer.

Gilda It's wrapped round the base of your spine. It's affecting your movement.

You keep forgetting.

Cole You don't *forget* – You don't *forget* / something like that –

Gilda It's a tumour.

Clark He forgot again –

Cole How long did I –

Gilda We just did the scan.

Clark You remember, don't you mate.

Gilda It's cancer –

Clark It's your turn to tell him.

Cole Tell me *what*?

Gilda It's wrapped round your spine.

Cole You shut your *mouth* –

Clark You've known for ages, mate.

Gilda I'm sorry –

Cole It's *nothing* –

Gilda Cole –

Cole I'm *fine* –

Gilda Just let us –

Cole You're / the ones –

Clark It's cancer.

Gilda It's wrapped round your spine.

Cole No, nonononono/ nonono –

Gilda / I'm sorry.

Clark Why can't he / remember?

Gilda Let us scan it –

Clark You keep forgetting.

Gilda It spread.

Cole / Both of you stop talking to me –

Gilda It's spreading –

Clark It's wrapped round your spine.

Cole Cut it –

Gilda We don't have the facilities to –

Cole Cut it *out of* / *me* –

Gilda / Cole –

Clark Calm down –

Gilda I'm sorry –

Cole YOU'RE LYING TO ME.

Gilda It's wrapped round your spine there's nothing we can do –

Clark He's gone again –

Cole You don't get to *tell* me this –

Clark His ear's going again –

Cole's *ear is bleeding.*

Gilda Cole –

Cole What's wrong with me? What is this?

Gilda Cole –

Cole Why am I walking like this –

Gilda I'm sorry –

Cole *Tell* me.

Clark He's gone / again.

Gilda Cole.

Cole You stay away / from me –

Clark Can he hear us?

Gilda / Cole –

Clark Cole –

Cole Make them come / get me.

Gilda Cole –

Cole You make them come and / get me – Call them, radio them, *fix* it –

Clark Cole –

Cole *collapses.*

Clark He's gone / again –

Gilda He's out of bed again –

Cole you're doing this to me . . .

Gilda Now / come on,

Clark Come on / mate –

Cole . . . stop doing this to me . . .

Gilda Can you hear us?

Clark He's pissed himself again –

Gilda Don't –

Cole what's wrong with my legs . . .

Gilda Cole –

Clark He's out of bed again –

Gilda You're sick –

Clark You're poorly mate –

Gilda You're not well –

You need to rest –

Are you tired?

Cole stop talking to me like that –

i'm not a –

He vomits.

what is this –

Gilda You're on drugs to make you better –

Clark Are you tired mate?

Gilda Let's go back to bed.

Cole stop it . . .

Clark *picks up* **Cole**. **Cole** *struggles.*

Clark It's alright –
Cole slow it down, stop, stop it, stop making it . . .
Gilda You just need to sleep –
Clark You'll feel better tomorrow –
Gilda Don't say that to him.
Cole *Stop it*. MAKE IT STOP.

They carry **Cole** *off to his room.*

We hear gabbling, wails, moans.

Clark *comes back on, unsettled.*

A silence.

Pause.

Gilda *comes back in.*

Pause.

Clark . . . Is he in the freezer now.

Gilda Yes, but don't . . .

Don't think about that.

Pause.

Clark How long do you think it was?

Gilda . . . I don't know.

Clark . . . Do you –

Do you think it was months, or *years* –

Gilda I don't know.

Pause.

Clark He just lay there the whole time, and we couldn't even –

Gilda We did the best we could.

. . .

We couldn't –

. . .

We did what we could.

Pause.

Clark He was a good captain.

Pause.

Gilda   He was / n't –

Clark   He was the –

Gilda   He wasn't the captain.

. . .

He was a meteorologist.

Clark   . . .

Gilda   He was a scientist. Like me.

Clark   . . . Yeah.

. . .

. . .

That's what I – I meant.

. . .

Pause.

Gilda   Are you alright?

Pause.

Clark   I don't know.

. . .

. . .

I can't . . .

. . .

I really feel like I'm hanging on by my nails here –

How long have you been standing there?

Gilda You're okay –

Clark I can't even tell if –

Gilda We'll do it together.

Clark . . .

Gilda We can help each other.

Clark . . .

Gilda Okay?

. . .

Start again.

Clark I don't get it.

Gilda Start again.

Clark I don't get what you mean –

Gilda Start again.

Clark I told you –

Gilda Tell it again. Tell me.

Pause.

Gilda You're in here.

Pause.

Clark I'm in here. It's – I'm sitting –

...

...

I see her at the window.

Gilda What's she look like.

Clark Like a – Person.

Gilda Small –

Clark Like a person looks.

Gilda Is she smiling?

Clark I can't see because of the – Reflection –

Gilda Then she disappears.

Clark She comes in –

Gilda You let her in.

Clark No, I – She –

Gilda She gets in here,

Clark I back away –

Gilda You're scared.

Clark I back away and fall,

Gilda And you're in here.

Pause.

Clark No.

Gilda No?

Clark No, that's not – That wasn't –

That wasn't mine.

Pause.

Gilda How about –
Clark Start again.
Gilda I have a ball.
Clark A ball.
Gilda I have a ball and you're working.
Clark I'm doing maths.
Gilda I'm bored.
Clark I need –
Gilda I don't like things that aren't real.
Clark I'm limping.
Gilda You're limping.
Clark My name is . . .
Gilda X
Clark I'm . . .

. . .

No.

Gilda Maths is for –
Clark No it's, this isn't –
Gilda I get further away.
Clark She gets further away.
Gilda I have a son
Clark Daughter
Gilda Who is . . .
Clark X

Gilda years
Clark Further away
Gilda To always make me tell
Clark X
Gilda For *years*
Clark leaving
Gilda You need a
Clark Computer science.
Gilda Calculator
Clark Left
Gilda X
Clark X

Pause.

Clark Carrr . . .
Gilda Carl –
Clark C – Cl – Cllarr –
Gilda X
Clark X
Gilda Co –
Clark Coa –
Gilda Coast –
Clark Coarse –
Gilda Claw –
Clark Claws –

Gilda X

Clark X

Gilda And the algorithm –

Clark Watch

Gilda Rain

Clark Rain

Gilda Rail

Clark X

Gilda And

– I'm in here

– It's

– I'm

– X

– at the window

– See

– X

– at the

– X

– at

– the girls

– she

– nothing

– mymother

– left

– *No.*

– X
– No.
– ...
– ...
– Start again –
– I'm in
– She
– X
– and
– all the –
–X
–X
–hear
–X
–not
–Where
–X
–Enough to
–lift
–X
–Punch the
–X
–crowd
–X
–X

–X

–X

–She

–South America

–South America

–South Amer

–South America

–she's

–X

–One the last

–pillarwebs

–Two

–She's

–X

–One in the freezer

–X in the freezer

–*Two* in the freezer –

–Two in the South Amer

–X

–in the fr

–X

–And

–And

–Birds

–Bird

–Birds

–X

–brush

–brushing

–brush against the

–X

–X

–X

– . . .

– . . .

–Glll –

–Glarr –

–X

–Luscin –

–Glllaah –

–Luscina –

–X

–Lus –

–Glll –

–G –

–G –

–da

–daaaaa

–X

–X

–X / X X X X X X X

–X X X X X X X X / X X X

–Everything

–X

–hold onto X

–hold onto / X in particu X she

–X X X X

–X X X X X X / X X X X X X X X X X X X X X X X

–X X X X X X X X X X X X X X X X / X X X X

–X X X X X / X X X X X X X X X X X X / X

–X

–X / X

–X

–X

X X X X X X X X X X X X X X X X X X X X X X X X X X X X X
X X X X X X X X X X X X X X X X X X X X X X X X X X X X X
X X X X X X X X X X X X X X X X X X X X X X X X X X X X X
X X X X X X X X X X X X X X X X X X X X X X X X X X X X X
X X X X X X X X X X X X X X X X X X X X X X X X X X X X X
X X X X X X X X X X X X X X X X X X X X X X X X X X X X X
X X X X X X X X X X X X X X X X X X X X X X X X X X X X X
X X X X X X X X X X X X X X X X X X X X X X X X X X X X X
X X X X X X X X X X X X X X X X X X X X X X X X X X X X X
X X X X X X X X X X X X X X X X X X X X X X X X X X X X X
X X X X X X X X X X X X X X X X X X X X X X X X X X X X X
X X X X X X X X X X X X X X X X X X X X X X X X X X X X X
X X X X X X X X X X X X X X X X X X X X X X X X X X X X X
X X X X X X X X X X X X X X X X X X X X X X X X X X X X X
X X X X X X X X X X X X X X X X X X X X X X X X X X X X X
X X X X X X X X X X X X X X X X X X X X X X X X X X X X X
X X X X X X X X X X X X X X X X X X X X X X X X X X X X X
X X X X X X X X X X X X X X X X X X X X X X X X X X X X X

[ ] 129

X

x x x x x x x x x x x x x x x x x x x x x x x x x x x x x x
x x x x x x x x x x x x x x x x x x x x x x x x x x x x x x
x x x x x x x x x x x x x x x x x x x x x x x x x x x x x x
x x x x x x x x x x x x x x x x x x x x x x x x x x x x x x

                          X

                          X

– . . .

– . . .

–X

– . . .

– . . .

–And I'm

– . . .

–X

– . . .

– . . .

– . . .

– . . .

–And I'm in here –

–I'm in

–X

—...
—...

–I'm

—...

—...
—...

Clark How long do you think.
Gilda I don't know. Even if we knew, we wouldn't know.
Clark ... Just *waiting* ...
Gilda Just like always.
Clark Waiting to die.
Gilda Don't say that.

—...

Clark It's been forever.

Gilda We don't know that.

Clark No one's ever going to come.
They're all gone. We're the last.

Gilda You're being –

Clark I just wish we knew. Then we could punch our cards right now –

Gilda That's enough.

Clark You should just put me in the freezer –

Gilda Stop it now.

Clark . . . with the others . . .

Gilda Come on. I can't talk to you if you're going to start blubbing every time –

Clark I'm not.

. . .

I'm not blubbing.

. . .

And if I was it'd be. . .

. . .

I'm allowed.

Gilda Is it because you thought you heard a ghost.

Clark I don't think I heard a ghost –

Gilda There's no such thing as ghosts.

Clark I know.

Gilda It's just the girls.

Clark The girls. Yeah.

Gilda Why don't we play a game or something.

Clark I wish you could tell me who I was.

Gilda You know who you are.

Gilda You know who you are.

Clark I wish I'd done lots of things different.

Gilda That's normal. You can't . . .

That's okay.

Clark . . . I wish I'd held my farts in more around you.

Gilda Well. You can start now.

Clark i'm leaving you all alone.

Clark you'll be all on your own out here.

that's the worst . . .

Clark i thought i could hold on longer.

. . .

but i can't.

. . .

i'm sputtering out.

. . .

my body's catching up with my brain.

Gilda It's alright.

Clark i don't want to leave you out here on your own, i can't –

Gilda I don't need you to look after me.

I'll be fine.

. . .

You just worry about yourself.

Clark what about my name.

Gilda What about it?

Clark . . .

Gilda We can have new names.

Clark . . . like what.

Gilda Well. It can be anything you want.

Clark . . .

. . .

Kratos.

Gilda Okay.

Okay Kratos.

Gilda Are you warm enough.

Clark . . . no.

Gilda How about now.

Clark did i kiss you once?

Gilda Yes. More than once.

Clark i thought maybe –

Gilda No. That was real.

Clark . . . can i do it again?

Clark that was nice.

Gilda Yes.

Clark i thought maybe i'd . . .

. . .

you laughed at my jokes.

Gilda Some of them.

Clark eventually.

. . .

i always fancied you.

. . .

i won you round.

Gilda Alright. Don't gloat.

Clark i'm so sorry . . .

Gilda Shush now.

Clark i'm sorry.

Gilda Just try and sleep.

Clark maybe they'll come

Gilda Maybe.

Maybe when you wake up they'll be here.

. . .

But either way I'll definitely be here.

. . .

I'm here.

. . .

You can count on me.

Kratos.

Clark all this time.

Clark   all this time i thought i was the main character.

Clark   x . . .

Gilda   X.

Clark   xo . . .

Gilda XO.

I

Gilda *is alone.*

II

Gilda *is alone.*
She mutters and talks to herself.

III

Gilda *is alone.*
She stands by the window looking out into the black.

IV

Gilda *is alone.*
She stands by the ladder, listening.
She climbs a few rungs tentatively.

V

A child's legs dangle from the hatch above.
Gilda *watches them.*

VI

Cole *leaves the room, visible only for a second.*
Gilda *doesn't see him.*

VII

Ray *stands by the window, blood streaming from*
the gash in his neck.
He and **Gilda** *watch each other.*

VIII

Gilda *cowers against a wall.*
A gigantic nightingale lies on the floor, injured, bleeding.
Gilda *appears the size of an infant next to it. She shrinks from the*
bird's laboured breathing.

IX

The machinery, the life systems, all have increased in volume tenfold.
Gilda *crouches on all fours howling in agony.*
The sound is deafening.
The walls run thick with blood.

The light slowly returns to the room.

Gilda *is still crouched on the floor.*

She tries to catch her breath.

The cupboard door under the sink swings open.

Gilda *watches as the* **Girl** *crawls out into the room backwards.*

She stands and turns around.

Her face is unscarred.

They consider each other.

Girl You didn't find me.

Pause.

Gilda No.

Pause.

Girl Do you give up?

Gilda *nods*.

Girl I was just in there. I hid in there.

Gilda Yes.

Pause.

Girl Well what is – What you have to – If you don't *find* me, then you have to, you have to do it again.

Because you didn't win.

Gilda Okay –

Girl And that's because you didn't find me again when I was up the ladder. I was up in there and you didn't find me as well.

Gilda No.

Girl So you just, just wait here and, and you have to count again and you can't look.

Gilda Okay –

Girl Just don't look then, don't look!

She runs to hide –

Gilda I – No – Wait – *Mattie.*

She stops.

Pause.

I can't . . .

. . .

I don't want to play this now.

. . .

I like to –

. . .

I like to know where you are.

Pause.

Young Mattie Are you sad again?
Gilda No, I'm –
I'm okay –

Young Mattie *goes and sits on* **Gilda** *heavily.*

Gilda Oof –
Young Mattie Why are you?
Gilda I'm not, I'm fine, I'm –
Young Mattie You're crying.

Gilda　I'm just – Don't do that please –

Young Mattie *is pressing her thumbs on* **Gilda**'*s eyes.*

Gilda　I just got mixed up.

I'm fine now I can see you.

Young Mattie　When can we play again though?

. . .

When I'm older?

Gilda　Maybe.

Pause.

Young Mattie　How old am I now do you think?

Pause.

Gilda　I don't know sweetheart.

. . .

Pause.

How old do you think I am?

Young Mattie　. . . Old. Really old.

Gilda　That's nice.

Young Mattie　Very old.

Gilda　Thank you.

148 X

Well why don't we measure ourselves, that'll tell us something.

Young Mattie Yes!

She runs over to one of the walls and stands excitedly against it –

Young Mattie I can see – It's bigger!

Gilda Where's your pencil.

Young Mattie It's in the –

Gilda We can't mark it without a pencil, can we.

Young Mattie You just – You just keep your hand where it's – Where how tall I am is –

Gilda I – Okay –

Young Mattie Hold it really still though –

Gilda Please.

Young Mattie Please –

She dashes from the room.

Pause.

Gilda *looks at the pencil marks.*

Gilda I don't need to –

. . .

We can just measure you again.

. . .

Mattie.

Pause.

She removes her hand.

She seems exhausted.

She pushes her hands through her hair, which greys as she does so, colour ebbing away.

Pause.

Mattie *comes in, an adult again*

She's brought pillows and blankets to set up a makeshift bed by the window.

Mattie Mum.

Gilda . . .

Mattie What?

Gilda . . . I thought you were in there.

. . .

Mattie I'm in here.

Gilda I thought I heard someone . . .

. . .

What's all this?

Mattie You said you wanted to be by the window.

Gilda . . .

Mattie Didn't you.

Gilda . . .

Mattie Mum.

Gilda Did you bring the pencil?

Mattie The pencil –?

Gilda To say how old you are.

Mattie I – Yes. We did that.

Gilda You saw how old?

Mattie I did.

Gilda You're always asking me.

Mattie I know. Let's –

Gilda I'm going to work out in space you know.

Mattie Yes –

Gilda I'm going to work off-world. I always wanted to.

Mattie You did.

Gilda Since I was tiny.

Mattie Come lie down for a bit.

Gilda *goes and gets into bed.*

Gilda Just be careful when you're out there.

Mattie I will.

Gilda And call me.

Mattie Okay.

Gilda I know you're busy but there's always time to call.

Mattie There is. How's that? Warm enough?

Gilda Are we still waiting?

Mattie No, we're not waiting for anything.

Gilda We're not?

Mattie No.

Gilda Oh.

. . .

Pause.

I don't know what time it is even.

. . .

And I can't see anything out this window.

. . .

I'm so useless aren't I.

Mattie Course not –

Gilda And I'm always *crying* –

Mattie That's okay.

Gilda It's pathetic.

Mattie It's allowed.

Pause.

Gilda I just thought –

I'd always have enough time.

To say all the things I wanted to say to you.

Mattie You don't need to –

Gilda I just wanted to tell you that I love you.

With *everything*.

Mattie I know.

Gilda It's so much it's the only thing that's left.

. . .

I can't remember half of anything but you're in all of it.

You're in everything.

All jumbled around.

. . .

. . .

And I was selfish.

Mattie Why?

Gilda Because.

I had you so I wouldn't be alone.

Mattie That's alright –

Gilda But I'm leaving you here –

Mattie It's okay –

Gilda You came to rescue me and I'm leaving you here –

Mattie Ssshh . . .

Gilda I don't want to leave you out here on your own, I can't bear it –

Mattie I'll be fine.

. . .

You just –

Worry about yourself.

. . .

. . .

Come on, I can't talk to you if you're blubbing all the time, can I?

Gilda I'm not blubbing.

Mattie No.

Me either.

Pause.

Gilda I'm tired.

Mattie I know.

Gilda So tired all the time.

Mattie Well don't go to sleep yet. Stay up and talk to me.

. . .

Tell me what it was like back there. Before.

Gilda You make me tell all that too much.

Mattie Alright, then –

Gilda And I can't remember it all.

Mattie Well then tell me about my father.

Gilda (*mock serious voice*) Your *father* . . .

Mattie What was he like.

Gilda I told you all that too.

Mattie Well tell me again.

Gilda . . .

He was annoying.

Mattie Annoying?

Gilda Very annoying.

And rude. And stupid.

. . .

More daft than stupid.

Mattie But you loved him.

Gilda Eventually.

I came around.

. . .

He was very scared.

. . .

He was scared I'd go first.

Pause.

Mattie Mum –

Gilda Mattie!

Mattie Wh –

Gilda Mattie –

Mattie I'm here, I'm –

Young Mattie *comes in.*

Young Mattie I'm here.

Gilda Did you do your teeth?

Young Mattie Yes.

Gilda If I give your mouth a sniff is it going to smell fresh?

Young Mattie I did them!

Gilda Okay then.

Mattie / I'm still . . .

Young Mattie   Can I sleep with you?

Gilda   I thought you liked your own bed.

Young Mattie (*shrugs*)   Only sometimes.

Gilda   Only sometimes. Alright.

Young Mattie *clambers into bed.*

Gilda   You warm enough?

Young Mattie   No . . .

Gilda   How about now. That's better isn't it.

Young Mattie   Yes.

Gilda   Yes.

Mattie   yes . . .

Pause.

Young Mattie   Mum?

Gilda   What?

Young Mattie   What was your mum like?

Gilda   You make me tell all that too much.

Young Mattie   I like it though.

Gilda   I'm too tired now.

Young Mattie   Please.

Pause.

Mattie please . . .

Beat.

Gilda My mother.

Was the last tree.

Beat.

Young Mattie / What did she look like?

Mattie what did she look like.

Gilda Big. Tall. She brushed against the sky.

She was filled with the most brilliant colour and light.

People came from all around to see her.

To hear her speak for the past.

. . .

And everyone would listen and listen, and cry and cry.

They'd ask every question they could think to ask.

And cry for what she told them.

For how things used to be.

. . .

Until eventually she couldn't speak anymore.

The colour and light faded.

And her leaves turned to dust.

. . .

So with her very last breath,

She lifted me here.

Away from what was left.

Sent to remember the rest.

. . .

. . .

. . . are you asleep?

. . .

Mattie . . . no . . .

Gilda *kisses her daughter goodnight.*

Gilda Sleep tight.

Pause.

Mattie . . . mum . . .

. . .

i'm still awake . . .

. . .

i'm still here . . .

. . .

. . .

i'm here . . .

. . .

i'm here . . .

. . .

i'm here . . .

. . .

158 X

i'm here . . .

. . .

i'm here . . .

As she repeats, we start to hear the ambient sound of a forest.

The birds sing and whistle to each other.

Then –

Black.

Notes

Nothing at all is visible out the window.

The clock above the window should run normally throughout each scene in Act One with the exception of **V** and **X**, where the glitches and breaks are marked.

In Act Two, Clark wears Ray's watch throughout.

Nothing should underline when time is speeding up, shifting, etc. The shifts in the dialogue are the only clues.

The nine short scenes found in Act Two should last longer than they perhaps appear to on the page.

The Glow

The Glow was first performed at the Royal Court Jerwood Theatre Downstairs, Sloane Square, on Monday 24 January 2022, with the following cast and creative team:

Fisayo Akinade
Rakie Ayola
Tadhg Murphy
Ria Zmitrowicz

Director Vicky Featherstone
Designer Merle Hensel
Lighting Designer Jessica Hung Han Yun
Composer & Sound Designer Nick Powell
Video Designer Tal Rosner
Movement Director Malik Nashad Sharpe
Assistant Director Rosie Thackeray

for Robert Holman,
who lit the way.

Cast of Characters

The Woman

Mrs Lyall
Mason

Haster

*All other characters to be played by the performers playing
Mrs Lyall, Mason, and Haster (see appendix).*

*To be played on an almost bare stage,
as much as possible conjured through light and shadow.*

Notes.

A question without a question mark denotes a flatness of tone.

- Indicates an interruption of speech or train of thought.
... Indicates either a trailing off, a breather, a shift, or a transition.
/ Indicates where the next line of dialogue interrupts or overlaps.
{ } Contains dialogue not heard by the audience.

I:
A Prominent Woman.

1.
1863.
An asylum. A cell without windows.
The Woman *sits on the ground, a shape in the shadows.*
Mrs Lyall *stands holding a lantern, the only source of light.*

Silence.

Mrs Lyall *lifts the lantern-*
The Woman *retreats slightly as the light touches her.*

Pause.

Mrs Lyall   Would you mind my taking a step closer?
So I might let the light find you?

Pause.

Mrs Lyall *moves to sit by* **The Woman**, *who retreats a little more.*

Mrs Lyall   Now now-
You've no need to be afraid.
…
Let's have a look at you-

She brings her hands to **The Woman's** *face and inspects her.*

Mrs Lyall   …I wonder.
Yes, I wonder what we might find under all of this.

She produces a handkerchief and begins wiping the grime from **The Woman's** *face.*

Mrs Lyall   Well now.
One wouldn't expect to find such a pretty young thing down here in the dark.

…
Do you have any idea as to how long you've been here?

The Woman   …*(Shakes head.)*

Mrs Lyall   Or perhaps who brought you here in the first?

The Woman   …*(Shakes head.)*

Mrs Lyall   Are you receiving any treatment at all?

The Woman   …

Mrs Lyall   Do the doctors or the porters come down here to see you?

The Woman   *(Shakes head.)*

Beat.

Mrs Lyall   Well how about a name.

The Woman   …

Mrs Lyall   You must have a name, at the very least.
That's something we're all given.

The Woman   …

Mrs Lyall   …Well how terrible for you.

Pause.

Mrs Lyall *drops the handkerchief to the ground.*

Mrs Lyall   My name–

Is Mrs Evelyn Lyall.
I am a prominent woman.
I am a writer, a social thinker, and a spiritualist medium of some renown.
And do you know-
Despite these achievements,
My own husband once tried to have me locked in a room very like this one.
So perhaps we're not so different, you and I.
…
Do you have any understanding, as to what a spiritualist medium is?

The Woman …*(Shakes head.)*

Mrs Lyall Well-
There is the world of matter- That which is seen.
And the world of the spirit- That which remains unseen by the great majority.
A medium conducts explorations into the latter.
…
I've come here in the course of my work.
And I feel so fortunate to have found you.
Do you know why?

The Woman *(Shakes head.)*

Mrs Lyall *stands.*

Mrs Lyall It has become clear to me that I am in need of an assistant.
I require a young, passive woman to amplify my own mediumship further.
I've spent the entire night searching this hospital for a suitable candidate and found none.
But now here we are.

…
Would you like to come home with me?

2.
The Lyall House, by candlelight.
Mrs Lyall *and* **Mason**.
Sadie *(The Woman) stands nearby, in the gloom.*

Mason   For how long?

Mrs Lyall   For as long as our work together requires.

Mason   Your 'work' requires she *live* here.
Even your coven would baulk at the very idea–

Mrs Lyall   I have disbanded my previous circle.

Mason   You repulsed them with your unsavoury obsessions.

Mrs Lyall   They lacked ambition.

Pause.

Mason   So this girl replaces them.

Mrs Lyall   And you shall join us.

Beat.

Mason   Absolutely not.

Mrs Lyall   That was not a request, Mason.

Mason   I won't collaborate in your sickness–

Mrs Lyall The circle must be at least three.

Mason So go drag another from the hole you found this one.
Better still, open the doors and invite the mudlarks in

Mrs Lyall I won't debate with you.

Mason And I won't live with some filthy woman you found in the gutter-
(To **Sadie**.*)* Don't *look* at me, Girl-

She looks at the floor.

Mrs Lyall I'll trust you not to be unkind to her.

Mason I will be as unkind as I like.
Do you think Father will approve of this?

Mrs Lyall I take no interest in your father's opinions.

Mason He'll set to having you-

Mrs Lyall If you share his beliefs you are welcome to follow him in seeking alternate accommodation.
It will of course mean a reduction in your allowance.

Mason …

Mrs Lyall *turns to* **Sadie**.

Mrs Lyall Mason will take you to your room now.

Mason I removed the cot from the scullery.

Mrs Lyall She will sleep in the room adjacent to mine.

Mason That's my room–

Mrs Lyall You may move your belongings to the third floor.

Mason …

Mrs Lyall *(To* **Sadie**.*)* Good night, my darling.
Pay no mind to Mason's behaviours, you are very welcome here.

Mrs Lyall *leaves.*

Silence.

Mason *stares at* **Sadie**.

Eventually he snatches a candlestick from a table.

Mason Come along then.

He goes to leave. **Sadie** *remains.*

Mason Come *along*.

She hurries after him as he leads her through hallways, upstairs, and down hallways darker still.

Mason I shall move my possessions from the room tomorrow; if you touch any of them I shall beat you.
When morning comes, do not open the shutters.
Like all ghouls my mother insists on darkness.
Now the servants have been dismissed doubtless *I* shall be expected to prepare your meals.
I have no interest in your preferences, you will eat what you are given.

He stops and turns to face her.

Mason This is not your home.
When Mother tires of you she shall toss you back where you were found.
Until then you stay out of my way, do you understand?
…
Are you *listening*, Girl?

Sadie Yyeesss-

Beat.

Sadie *looks quickly to her feet, unnerved by the cracked bark of her voice.*

Mason *stares at her a moment longer before removing a candle from the stick and thrusting it at her.*

Mason Here.
Down the hall.

He leaves.

Sadie *stands alone in the dim light of the candle.*

She looks around.

She makes her way slowly down the hall, feeling her way.

We listen to her nervous breathing.

We hear a heavy footstep nearby-

Another-

Someone is approaching in the dark.

Sadie *lifts the candle and watches as a* **Knight** *in bloodied armour steps into the light.*

They consider each other.

The candle goes out.

3.
Mrs Lyall *lights a candle. There is a table without chairs.*
Sadie *stands nearby.*

Mrs Lyall   Sadie.

Sadie *is distracted, looking off and away.*

Mrs Lyall   Sadie.

Sadie   Yes.

Mrs Lyall   You're not yet used to your new name.
Is it clear what's expected of you this evening.

Sadie   …

Mrs Lyall   I don't relish repeating myself, Sadie.

Sadie   I hearrdd voices.

Mrs Lyall   Voices. Whose voices?

Sadie   I donn't…
…
I don'tt-

Enter **Mason**.

Mason   I refuse to cook for her.
She wouldn't touch a thing I prepared.

Mrs Lyall   Perhaps if you prepared something edible, Mason.

Mason   It's not enough you give her my room, you'll have me serve as her *maid-*

Mrs Lyall   That's quite enough theatrics for now.
I must retire to calibrate myself and quiet is essential whilst I do so.
Imagine the volume I might prefer your voice to be at, then lower it still.

Mrs Lyall *leaves.*

Mason   …an evening with my mother and the dead.
How did my social life plunge to such depths.

Sadie *watches as* **Mason** *pours himself a drink.*

Mason   I don't like being stared at, Girl.

Sadie   …wwerre you aafrraidd?

Mason   Is your tongue as slow as the rest of you?

Sadie   …

Mason   Afraid of what.

Sadie   The ffirst timme Mrs Lyall-
Ttethered your ssoul to herrs.

Mason My mother never 'tethered her soul' to mine.
Parents traditionally don't use their children in demonic rituals.
Did your own ever use you to raise the dead?

Sadie I ddon't remember. My parents.

Mason I imagine you would had they shared my mother's interests.

Sadie …I-

Mason What is that.

Sadie …

Mason What are you fiddling with there.

Sadie …

Mason Show me.

Sadie …

Mason *Show* me.

Sadie *has a small stuffed horse.*

Pause.

Mason …Give that to me.

Sadie …

Mason It is mine. Give it to me.

Sadie I ffffound it-

Mason In my room. Give it here.

Sadie …

Mason *Give* it.

Sadie No.

Beat.

Mason *strides across the room and snatches the horse.*

Sadie No-

Mason Did I not tell you to leave my belongings untouched? Are you *deaf?*
You touch my things again and I'll have you replaced with some other damaged girl-

Mrs Lyall *has returned in a new dress.*

Mrs Lyall Mason, I won't have you bullying her.

Mason She is *stealing* from me-

Mrs Lyall What use can you have for that old thing?

Mason She stole my room and now she steals my possessions-

Mrs Lyall If she wants it for company at night what harm can that-
Mason-

Mason *has ripped the horse in two and throw the pieces to the ground.*

Mason There. Now there are no jealousies.

He goes to leave-

Mrs Lyall Mason really- *Mason.*
We are ready to begin.

Sadie *is inspecting the torn horse.*

Mrs Lyall You will make peace with Sadie and clear this atmosphere.
The spirits favour a light, welcoming air.

Mason Then they would do well to visit another house.

Mrs Lyall Now come along.

Mason …She's staring at me.

Sadie's *eyes are fixed coldly on* **Mason**.

Mrs Lyall Mason was acting out in a juvenile manner, we shan't take it to heart, shall we Sadie.

Sadie *continues to stare.*
Something is shifting in the room's atmosphere.

Mason Stop-
Looking at me like that-

Mrs Lyall Besides, you're a grown woman. You've no need for a child's toy, have you.
Have you, Sadie.

Mason Tell her to stop.
…
/Stop- Stop this-

Mrs Lyall Sadie.
...
Sadie.

Sadie *turns away and goes to* **Mrs Lyall's** *side.*

Mrs Lyall There.

Mason Did you see how she looked at me–

Mrs Lyall We are moving on with our evening.

Mason She-

Mrs Lyall Mason you will take your place at the piano without further complaint.

Beat.

Mason *retreats to a piano in the corner of the room.*
Mrs Lyall *takes* **Sadie's** *hand.*

Mrs Lyall Now Sadie, you are excused from singing of course until you become familiar with the words. For now, just try and contribute to a bright, positive aura.
Are we ready?

Mason *starts playing.*

Mrs Lyall There we are.

Mrs Lyall *begins to sing–*

>   Only a thin veil between us–

Mrs Lyall I shan't be a lone voice–

Mason *joins-*

> My loved ones so precious and true-

Mrs Lyall If you could find a little more enthusiasm-

> Only as mist before sunrise,
> I am hidden away from your view-

Mrs Lyall *Much* better- Maintaining this level-

> Often I come with my blessing,
> And strive all your sorrows to share-

Sadie *becomes distracted as a strange echo laps at the walls.*

> At night when you're quietly sleeping,
> I kiss down your eyelids in prayer-

Soon, it's as if the scene has been plunged underwater.

Mrs Lyall And onto the chorus-

She looks up as the sound of a bird calling breaks through the fog.

> Only a thin veil between us,
> Some morning the angels will come,
> And then in a bright land of beauty-
> We'll gather with loved ones at home,
> At home-

Just as she's about to panic, the scene rushes back to the surface, and **Sadie** *joins in with the song, her voice a manic yell-*

Mrs Lyall *and* **Mason** *gradually stop singing and playing to watch her.*

> Home, beautiful home,
> No longer in sadness alone,
> But safe, in the kingdom of glory,
> We'll dwell, with the loved ones at home-

Pause.

Mrs Lyall That's-
Very good, Sadie.
…
You should have mentioned you knew the words.

Pause.

Mrs Lyall If I could ask you to take your place.

Sadie *clambers up onto the table and lies down.*
Mrs Lyall *moves to the head of the table, placing her hands around* **Sadie's** *skull.*

Mrs Lyall Mason.

Mason *moves to the other end of the table.*
He reluctantly takes hold of **Sadie's** *feet.*

Mrs Lyall And now we'll make it known to whomever might be present here this evening that you are welcome, and that we await any communication you might send us with patience and open arms. And Sadie, as we discussed- You will clear your mind and allow yourself to become completely passive whilst we wait.

Mason An irony that your power is to render yourself powerless.

Mrs Lyall Thank you, Mason.

Sadie MMMrs Lyalll-

Mrs Lyall Hush now, Sadie.

Mrs Lyall *settles in for a long wait.*

A long time passes.

A clock in the next room chimes the hour.

A long time passes.

A long time.

Mason …How much longer must we-

A loud thump from somewhere. **Mason** *jumps.*

Mrs Lyall Here we are.

Sadie *seems uneasy.*

Mrs Lyall Good evening to you, Spirit.
If you would bear with me whilst we establish a simple system of communication-

If we could agree on a single rap for a 'yes' and two raps for a 'no', would that be acceptable to you?

Pause.

A thump. Softer, this time.

Mrs Lyall Splendid.
Are you alone this evening?

Pause.

Another thump. Softer, still.

Mrs Lyall Very good.
Are you a former tenant of this house?

Pause.

Two thumps.

Mrs Lyall No. Then-

Another-

Mrs Lyall No-
If you could try and keep to the system /we agreed-

Mason How are you doing that?

Mrs Lyall Quiet-

Mason   Where is it coming from?

Mrs Lyall   *Quiet-*

Sadie   Mmrs Lyall-

Mrs Lyall   Did you pass-

Sadie   I cann'tt-

Mrs Lyall   Did you pass before your time-

A very long scraping of fingernails on board-

A moment.

Then a colossal bang-

Sadie *is hyperventilating.*

Mrs Lyall   Sadie-

Mason   What is this?

An extremely loud thump-

Mason   Mother, stop-

Mrs Lyall   Rest, spirit, rest-

More thumps, scraping, louder-

Mrs Lyall   How might we converse if you insist on-

Silence.

A long scream pulls out of **Sadie**-
Starved of oxygen at first, it rises from a rasp to a roar-
She leaps up from the table, thrashing-

Mrs Lyall   Hold her- *Hold her-* The Spirit has her-

They try and restrain **Sadie** *as the crashing continues, louder-*

Mrs Lyall   *Hold* her Mason-

Mason   I'm /trying-

Sadie   meam lucem demere conantur- meam lucem demere conantur!

4.
Mason *is watching the front of the house from an upstairs window. The last of the day's light crosses the room through the open shutter.*

Enter **Mrs Lyall**.

Mrs Lyall   Have they left.

The bell rings downstairs.

Mrs Lyall   …How many are they.

Mason   Two. And a third with the carriage.

Pause.

Mason   They're leaving.

Pause.

Mason *comes away from the window.*

Mason   Who is she?

Mrs Lyall She is nobody. She means nothing to no one.

Mason Clearly that's not the case if they're sending men to retrieve her.

Mrs Lyall They held no record of her even being there. She was abandoned in an unused cell. I doubt she'd seen another for years.

Mason Someone must have been feeding her-

Mrs Lyall She is *no* one.

Mason Then send her back and find another-

Mrs Lyall Absolutely not. I paid more than handsomely for her-

Mason You paid a porter for silence whilst you stole her-

Mrs Lyall I did not 'steal' anything-

Mason You can find another.
One more tolerable to live with-
One who doesn't talk to herself at all hours- Spend all night clattering about in the library-

Mrs Lyall You have made your dislike for her clear.

Mason Any number of women can perform your table rappings for you-

Mrs Lyall You would call what I brought to pass table rappings?

Pause.

Mrs Lyall Sadie is a perfect conduit for my powers.
I could never hope to find another as attuned.
I brought a spirit *into* her body.
You heard how she spoke.

Mason She spoke in Latin. She is performing for you, to stay in your favour-

Mrs Lyall How could she know such a language?
Without education?

Mason You don't know what education she has-
You don't know anything about her-

Mrs Lyall What did she say.

Beat.

Mason …I failed Latin.

Mrs Lyall I am aware of your failures, Mason.

Pause.

Mason Light.
…something about- Stealing her light.

Pause.

Mrs Lyall They are not coming for her.
Your father's lifestyle has once again extended beyond what I give him.
He has likely begun a second campaign to have me removed from control of my accounts.

Mason So stop these acts which give him fuel to-

Mrs Lyall You might sooner ask I stop breathing.
What I could have achieved by now, had so much of my time not been spent hiding money from men.
I am about to make all distinctions of flesh irrelevant.
To birth the new age of the spirit.
I will not allow small-mindedness to threaten that.
…
And if it be the case they are pursuing her, soon there will be no one left to claim.
I shall fill Sadie with the ancient spirit of another in *per*manence.
What little there is of her shall be erased.
Then your father and any others intent on containing me will *kneel* before me.
…
They cannot lock away a proven necromancer.

Pause.

Mrs Lyall I can smell the drink on you.
I need your wits sharp.

Mrs Lyall *leaves.*

Mason *mops his brow.*

Sadie *is stood in the shadows, holding a book.*

Mason *sees her and jumps.*

Mason How long have you been standing there?
…
Go to your room.

Sadie What's wrong with you?

Mason Nothing. Nothing is wrong with me.
A fine question for *you* to ask.

He closes the window shutter.

Sadie Who was outside?

Mason No one.

Sadie You were talking about me.

Beat.

Mason You think we have nothing better to discuss than you? Go to your room, you'll need rest if you're to perform tonight.

Sadie I don't want to do it again.

Mason I dare say it's not up to us.

Sadie It hurts.

Mason You don't need to maintain your act around me.
…
What are you clutching-

He snatches her book.

Sadie Poems-

Mason Tennyson. Knights and grails and nonsense.
A little advanced for you, isn't it?
Last I knew you were reading fairy tales.

Sadie Give it back now.

Mason   This quest of yours for education is a waste of time.
One can dress a dog in finery- It is still a dog.
All night I hear you talking to yourself in the library-
Don't you sleep?

Pause.

Mason   You don't sleep?

Pause.

Mason   …You don't sleep.

Pause.

Sadie   Give my book back now.

Pause.

Mason   It is not 'your' book.
You do not own any books.
You own nothing.
You are squatting in my home. Reading *my* books.
Taking advantage of *my* mother's desperation to-
I *told* you-

Sadie *is reaching for the book-*
Mason *grabs her wrist-*

There's a flash, and we're suddenly on a scorched battlefield, the ground soaked with blood. Fires blaze nearby.
We make out the shadows of warring men, the cries of fury and pain.

Mason *looks around in panic-*
He lets go of **Sadie's** *wrist-*

Instantly we're back in the Lyall house.

Pause.

Mason *stares at* **Sadie**, *who is breathing heavily. He drops the book and flees.*

Sadie *recovers herself.*

She picks the book up and clamps it to her chest, muttering to herself inaudibly.

Sadie *continues to whisper. We only catch occasional words.*	**Sadie** {-and when riding across the land he meets a woman on a shining white horse come away come away she called to him and her beauty was so great he fell in deepest love and climbed onto the back of her horse and they rode across the fields and the hills until they reached the sea and kept riding until they rode across the surface of the water and under the waves to a magical kingdom where all was well where there were no wars and no disease and they were married and lived happily together-}
She hears something and looks off-	
She puts the book down and walks towards the sound, away from the candlelight.	
We listen to her whispering as she walks.	
The sounds of wildlife as dull light creeps through a canopy of leaves- We are in a forest.	

A **Man** *in animal hides is hunched in the dirt, his back to her.*

He turns and sees her.

He stands, clutching a rock.

I: A Prominent Woman   191

He looks her up and down.

He steps towards her-

> **Sadie** *reaches out her hand-*
> *A bright spark of light ignites in her palm, hovering.*

The **Man** *stops and stares at it, fearful.*

Pause.

Sadie *is seized from behind by* **Aulus**, *a Roman Soldier-*

The spark dies, the **Man** *and the forest vanish-*

Sadie *struggles with* **Aulus** *as he tries to restrain her-*

Aulus   noli te moveri-

Sadie *manages to get on top of* **Aulus** *and wrap her hands around his skull-*

We begin to hear a voice from somewhere-

Mrs Lyall   *(From off.)* Sadie...

Aulus *grunts in pain as* **Sadie's** *fingers push into his flesh-*

Mrs Lyall   *(From off.)* Sadie-

Sadie   ego sum lux-!

She leans down and rips **Aulus'** *nose away with her teeth, spitting it out- Blood sprays as he yells-*

Mrs Lyall   Spirit- Release!

Mrs Lyall *pulls* **Sadie** *away from* **Mason** *as he screams and clutches his face-*

Sadie *looks on with horror as* **Mason** *flees the room.*

Sadie I saw him…

Mrs Lyall That's alright, my darling.

Sadie I saw him-

Mrs Lyall Don't fret now-
My clever darling…
My clever girl…

Mrs Lyall *cradles* **Sadie**, *stroking her hair.*

5.
Mrs Lyall *cradles* **Sadie** *in a dim pool of candlelight.*

Mrs Lyall To think the condition I found you in-
And now look at you.
Part of the most important work of the century.

Sadie I hurt him…

Mrs Lyall Mason will recover.

Sadie I thought he was someone else…

Mrs Lyall You are so passive the spirits will flock to you.
It can be overwhelming.
Be assured I am in control the entire time.

Sadie I don't think they're spirits.

Beat.

Mrs Lyall Well you are uneducated in these matters. You shall trust my judgement.

Sadie Feels like- Hands.
In my skull.
And I see things.

Mrs Lyall What do you see.

Sadie I can't make sense of it.

Mrs Lyall Let me help you.

Pause.

Sadie …blood.
…pain.
…
Holes in the ground filled with the dead.
Men hung flaming on chains.
People spread open on the ground.
…
I see myself at the head of a great army.
Stood on a battlefield soaked with ruin.
I see them all at once from a great height.
Piled up. Piles. Bloated. Rotted. Looking-
Looking at me.
Pulling at my feet.
Wanting things from me.
And I can't give them what they want.
So they hate me.
And I hate them.
Even you.
Sometimes I look at you and I hate you, too.

You're the same as the rest.

Pause.

Mrs Lyall I don't want anything from you, Sadie.

Sadie Yes you do.

Pause.

Mrs Lyall I want to help you.
To elevate you.
I want to water you until you bloom.
…
These are dreams. Phantoms.
Perhaps there are parts of your past muddled amongst them, but what does it matter?
You are here with me now.
None of it matters.
Aren't you happy here?

Sadie …

Mrs Lyall You are in a rare position in life.
Most people are so terribly alone.
It is a grotesque fate to be born human.
Trapped within one's self in a cage of flesh.
…
You and I are forging a bond to transcend that curse.
Our spirits shall be twinned.
Stitched together with cords of brilliant light.
Doesn't that sound wonderful?

Sadie …I want to know who I am.

Mrs Lyall You are my darling Sadie.
Whoever you were before is an irrelevance.
I named you anew, and soon I shall gift you a new soul to match.
This person you have been has brought you nothing but pain. We shall replace her with another.
So you might have a new life.
And when the world knows me as the woman who tore the veil between worlds, my power shall be absolute.
And you will be there by my side.
My spirit daughter.

Beat.

Mason *bursts in, drunk. Where his nose was is now a bloody hole.*

Mason If you require dinner I shan't be making any.

Mrs Lyall Mason you will bandage yourself, I won't have you dripping throughout the sitting.

Mason You won't have to suffer my presence at all this evening Mother, I shall not be participating.

Mrs Lyall You're drunk.

Mason Not half as much as I'd care to be.

Mrs Lyall I ask so little of you-

Mason You ask the *Earth*.
You ask I share my home with this thing-

Sadie Don't call me that-

Mason You ask I tolerate being *mutilated-*

Mrs Lyall Such melodrama-

Mason *Look* at me.
I could charge ad*mission* for this.

Sadie I didn't mean to- I thought you were someone else-

Mrs Lyall /You see?

Mason *Who?!* Who did you think I was?!
…
I won't work in your morgue a minute longer-

Mrs Lyall I shan't allow your cowardice to stall my progress-
My powers will not be suppressed-

Mason You *have* no powers.

Pause.

Mason You're a fraud.
The worst kind of fraud. Unaware you are one.
There is no such thing as a spiritual medium.
…
It's her.
…
She-
Is…Something.

Pause.

Mason She doesn't eat. She doesn't sleep.
She causes- *Things* to occur-

Mrs Lyall That's enough.

Mason   She is something *other*.
You should never have brought her into this house.
She was locked away for a reason.
…
You see how she looks at me?

Mrs Lyall   We are both looking at you with displeasure.

Pause.

Mason *grabs* **Sadie** *by her clothing-*

Sadie   /Let go-

Mrs Lyall   Mason-

Mason   If you refuse to evict her, I shall do it for you-

Mrs Lyall   /Put her down-

Sadie   Let go of me-

Mason   She's lucky I'm being so lenient- We should burn her at the stake-!

Sadie *pushes her finger into* **Mason's** *wound-*
As he screams she presses her face to his-

Mason *vanishes.*

Silence.

Mrs Lyall *walks about the room, then off, looking for* **Mason**.
Sadie *stands stock still, breathing heavily.*

Mrs Lyall *returns.*

Pause.

The Woman I sent him away.

Pause.

Mrs Lyall Sadie-

The Woman I won't help you anymore.

Mrs Lyall You are to wait for my instruction before conducting any-

The Woman I know who I am.

Pause.

The Woman I saw-

Mrs Lyall You are nothing, Sadie.
…
You are waste.
Thrown away like spoiled meat.
Your sole value is the role I have given you.
You are a tool for my using. An empty vessel I will fill however I choose.
…
But now you're convinced of your importance, is that it?
You perform one crude vanishing act and think you can usurp me?
You are a woman of great significance.
To be feared.

Pause.

Mrs Lyall *strides across the room and seizes* **Sadie** *by the wrist-*

The Woman No-

Mrs Lyall You will sit and perform your duty, Sadie-

The Woman That's not my name-

Mrs Lyall Then what shall I call you? Wretch? Traitor?
You deny me once more and I'll toss you into a hole far darker
than the one I found you in.
I'll make sure the light *never* finds you.

The Woman I *am* the light!

Pause.

The Woman I'll give you what you want.
I will bring death here.
I'll give it all to you.
I'll show you how much pain one soul can endure.

Beat.

Mrs Lyall *breaks one of* **The Woman's** *fingers. She howls in pain.*

Mrs Lyall If you insist on behaving as a beast, I will treat you as one-

She breaks another.

Mrs Lyall How dare you speak to me this way-
You will be quiet and do as you are told, or I will clip your wings
further-

She wrenches **The Woman** *back to her feet-*

Mrs Lyall You've wasted enough of my time.

Hold still-

The Woman *begins to glow.*

Mrs Lyall *steps back in surprise.*

Mrs Lyall   …No- No more of these vulgar displays-

The Woman *watches her fingers snap back into place.*

She turns her attention back to **Mrs Lyall**.

We hear heavy footsteps approaching.

The **Knight** *emerges from the shadows behind* **The Woman**.

Mrs Lyall   Oh- Oh my…

He draws his sword.

Mrs Lyall *falls to her knees.*

The Woman *stands over her.*

Mrs Lyall   Oh my…

The Woman *vomits a glowing lava into* **Mrs Lyall's** *mouth.*

She chokes and splutters in panic, clawing at her throat and face.

The Woman *and the* **Knight** *fade away into the black as it closes in-*

6.
343 AD.
Mrs Lyall *writhes on the ground, hacking and coughing.*

We hear **The Woman** *screaming- Somewhere far away, in terrible pain.*

Mrs Lyall *sits up with difficulty and looks around at the darkness.*

The Woman   *(Off.)* meam lucem demere conantur...!

We hear someone approaching.

Aulus *is here, lit by a nearby fire.*

There's a hole where his nose should be.

Aulus phantasma...

He draws his sword-

Mrs Lyall   Oh- Oh no-

Black.

II:
Fisher King.

1.
1348.
A dungeon.
Haster *(The Knight) stands holding a torch, the sole source of light. He stares into the dark, waiting.*
We hear a shifting of chains.

The Woman *steps forward into the light.*
She wears a huge iron collar, strung with chains leading off in all directions.

She and **Haster** *consider each other.*

2.
By a small fire, **Haster** *chews on a hunk of salted meat.*
The Woman *watches.*

Pause.

The Woman Where are we going?

Pause.

The Woman You won't say?

Pause.

The Woman You'll take me from a place and not say where…

Pause.

The Woman Is it far?

Pause.

The Woman How many days will it take to get there?

Pause.

Haster Many.

Pause.

The Woman But how many, though?

Haster There is no number.

Pause.

The Woman …but if you were to guess a number.

Pause.

The Woman If you were to pack enough meat for the journey, how many days meat would-

Haster Do you feel pain.

The Woman …Yes.

Haster Then stop your tongue lest I cause you to feel some.

Pause.

Haster I am taking you south.
…
To the King.

Pause.

The Woman Why?

Haster   You are his property.

The Woman   I'm no one's property-

Haster   You are of this land. You are his to own.

The Woman   Are you his property, too?

Pause.

The Woman   What does he want with me?

Haster   It is not your concern.

The Woman   It is my concern- It's *me*. I am my concern.

Pause.

The Woman   I know who you are.

Pause.

The Woman   I heard your stories.
They use them to scare children.
…
'If you don't get to sleep, Lord Haster'll come and take your heads off!'

She grins.

Pause.

The Woman   They tell stories of me, too.

Haster   I hold no belief in them.

The Woman …Well I don't believe yours.

Haster *fixes her with a stare, then drinks from a bladder of water.*

The Woman You're hard to talk to.

Haster I have no desire to speak to you.

The Woman Do you ever desire to speak to anyone?
…
Would you ever give greetings to a person?
Or say 'Goodbye!'
…
…No one spoke to me there, either.
Where you found me.
…
They were afraid of me.
They kept me in more chains than a- A beast would need.
…
They wouldn't even look at me when they brought my meals.
…
And they brought me meals on every day, though I never took one bite.
Nor one sip of water.
Or wine.
…
Nor goats milk.
…
Nor mead.
…
Nor broth.
…
Nor the juice of-

Haster *Stop naming fluids.*
…

Did I not tell you to shut your hole?
…
I am taking you south.
No words will change your course.
Until we reach-

The Woman *jumps up and flees into the woods.*

Haster   Wh- Hold- Woman!

Haster *struggles to his feet and after her-*

Haster   *Woman!*

He blunders wildly through the trees, changing directions repeatedly, soon lost.

He's moved too far from the fire, and the moonlight has deserted him.

We listen to his breathing, his faltering steps.

Haster   *Woman!*

Haster *walks on in total darkness.*

Eventually we hear someone approaching-

Len- *an ARP Warden- illuminates* **Haster** *with his hooded lantern.*

The two look at each other, dumbfounded.

An air raid siren begins to wail- **Haster** *backs away into the dark-*

Len   'Ere- You- Stop!

Haster *hurries away as the siren shifts in tone and length-*

A fluorescent strip light snaps into life above him-

He's in a tiled observation room.

The Woman *is here, ripping electrodes with long trailing wires from her body and skull. An alarm blares- A* **Figure** *in a fallout suit enters the room-*

Haster *stumbles away in fear as the light snaps off.*

He's running now, panicked-

Dim light far off in the distance casts strange shadows-

We can see figures hurrying about, we hear whispering- **The Woman's** *voice?*

Haster *draws his sword-*

Snatches of piano warp through the air.

We see a light coming near-

The Woman *steps into view.*

She is glowing.

3.
1993.
Ellen's *house.*
The Woman *stands caught under the hallway light.*

Ellen   Can I help you?

The Woman   …

Ellen Are you lost?

The Woman   …

Ellen Hm?

The Woman   …I didn't think anyone lived here-

Ellen So you just thought you'd come inside?

The Woman The grass was long-

Ellen Never you mind how long the grass is-
The grass being long doesn't mean you can just come into someone's house.
…
I was planning on cutting it tomorrow if you must-
Never you mind how long it is.
Can you imagine what that feels like? Hearing someone breaking into your home.

The Woman The door wasn't locked-

Ellen Do you do this a lot?
Waltz into people's houses? Help yourself?

The Woman …Sometimes.

Ellen You do?

The Woman Only if they're not there.
I don't take anything.
I'm not a thief.

Ellen So what are you then?

Pause.

Ellen   What's your name.

The Woman   …

Ellen   You don't have a name-?

The Woman   Brooke.

Ellen   Brooke.
Well, Brooke. Can you give me a reason why I shouldn't call the police?

Brooke   …

Ellen   Hm?

Brooke   …I-

4.
1348.
Woods.
The first light of dawn creeps through the trees.
Haster *tackles* **The Woman** *to the ground.*

The Woman   Let go- Let go of me-

Haster   Try and lose me with trickery?

The Woman   You followed me-

Haster   What was that- What was it?

The Woman   I can't control it- You said you don't believe-

Haster   *I do not!*

Pause.

Haster   I have no belief in magic, nor spirits, nor gods-
And I have no belief in *you*.
I believe only in *death*, and I will visit it upon you until it *sticks* if you lead me astray again.

The Woman   I'm not afraid of you-

Haster   Nor I you, Girl.

5.
1979.
Evan's *Room.*
A tatty lamp shows us how dingy and cluttered it is.

Evan   Man I'm glad to see you. Like, I'm glad to see anyone, you know? A *person*.
I haven't left this room in I don't even know- I heard you knocking and I was like 'What's that?', Like I didn't recognise the sound- Like I'd forgotten other people existed, you know? I get so wrapped up in what I'm doing sometimes-

The Woman   I found your leaflet-

Evan   Newsletter, yeah, you said. I'm actually surprised there's still some of those knocking around- Where'd you find it?

The Woman   In the library. In a book about- About ghosts.

Evan   Spiritualism man, yeah. Nice.
I actually don't do that anymore- Leave them in library books like that.

I kept getting mentals coming here. They'd find them and think
I was sending them secret messages- Which in a way I was. This
guy showed up once without a shirt on talking about satellites
and then he got his cock out. Made me think I should change my
approach.
Also I kept getting in trouble with librarians.
You said you're researching-

The Woman I have a degree.

Evan You're- You're doing a degree?

The Woman Yes. Yes.

Evan Right. Well- You know- Be careful.
I got kicked out of uni for writing about this stuff.
Kicked out slash dropped out.

The Woman Why?

Evan Academics don't consider it history.

The Woman What do they consider it.

Evan Folklore. Myth. You know-
Shite, depending on who you ask.
But- And I've always said this-
You go back far enough and everything turns to myth. You know?

The Woman ...No.
...
You don't look like a historian.

Evan Oh- Like- What's a historian meant to look like?

The Woman Just- Different. To you.

Evan Well I actually consider myself part of a new wave of historians.
The old guard are all washed up-
They talk about the Tudors and Victorians the same way they talk about the dinosaurs. Like they're dead.

The Woman They are dead.

Evan No, man. They're all still here. Like static.
We're wrapped *around* them.

6.
1993.
Brooke *and* **Ellen** *are watching TV.* **Ellen** *knits.*
She steals glances at **Brooke** *every now and then.*

Narrator *(TV.)* -multiple skulls with head trauma suggesting tribal conflict in the area.

Academic *(TV.)* Several communities made homes here due to the proximity of the river, with the nearby forestland providing essential fuel and sustenance.

Narrator *(TV.)* Simple flint tools suggest a rapidly developing people determined to impose their will-

Ellen *turns the TV off.*

Pause.

Ellen Did you wipe the tiles down afterwards?

Brooke Yes.

Ellen   …Well you look better for a wash.
…
I can't get you to eat anything.

Brooke   No.

Ellen   Nothing to drink.

Brooke   *(Shakes head.)*

Pause.

Ellen   Is there somewhere I can drive you.
Do you have somewhere-

Brooke   I'm not from anywhere.

Ellen   Everyone's from somewhere.

Pause.

Ellen   You've a face on you for someone who's been let into a warm house on a cold night.
…
You don't like me, you've decided?
…
Or you don't like anyone.
…
Everyone's the same to you.
Suit yourself.
We'll have the television back on.
That's what people do when they run out of things to say to each other.

She turns the TV back on and goes back to knitting.

This time **Brooke** *is the one stealing glances.*

Academic *(TV.)*   -these statuettes we found here seem to represent a matriarchal society built in the image of a goddess-

7.
1979.
Evan *is showing* **The Woman** *various books and papers.*

Evan   So this is like a pretty standard place to start. Your meat and two veg. Here's Henry Six, middle of the fifteenth century, back end of the hundred years war, no one can be fucked anymore, everyone just wants done with it- So he goes and marries Margaret of Anjou, who is French.
Here's a painting of the wedding- Nice spread and everything, all your lords and ladies here, and-

The Woman   There.

Evan   Wh- Yeah. That's ah- Yeah. Good eye.
She looks a bit different each time but you can always tell it's her. How she's drawn, or stitched or whatever- Slightly apart from the rest, this sort of glow around her- Classic.
So for ages people were like, who *is* that, you know- So-

The Woman   I already know this.

Evan   Oh-

The Woman   Your leaflet-

Evan   Newsletter.

The Woman   It wasn't talking about this, it was saying how-

Evan I'm just building a story here- Like an overview for you-
But I'll speed it up a bit if you're gonna-
Here-
This is from earlier- Edward Three.
Still got the glow around her, but this time she's kind of a monster-
(Reading.) 'And chains of iron were shackled to the demon's throat.
And the demon held no hunger. Nor thirst.
Nor did it ever know sleep'.

The Woman This isn't what you said-

Evan I'm just showing you how she's different every time.
Sometimes she's a demon or a witch or something, and sometimes she's like a Mother Nature kind of thing- But really she's always kind of the same-
Here she is in the King's procession-
Here she is at war-
Here she is as a kind of a fairy-
Here she is being cut to pieces-
Here she is being burnt at the stake-

The Woman Where are the others?

Beat.

Evan What?

The Woman You said- You wrote about them-
You said there were women who never slept, women who-

Evan Woman. Singular.

Pause.

The Woman   …There are no others.

Evan   No, like–
That's kind of the point of the book–

He holds out a battered old book.

Evan   *The* Woman.
The Woman in Time.

Pause.

The Woman *takes the book and looks at it.*

Evan   That's where all this comes from. What my newsletters are about.
…I'm sorry if I phrased something weird or made you think–
Like if I confused you–
…
Are you alright?

A roll of thunder that only **The Woman** *can hear.*

8.
1348.
A hilltop. Rain.
Haster *strikes a fire into life whilst* **The Woman** *watches, her wrists bound.*
The rain eases.

Catch *is stood nearby.*

Catch   Share your heat?

Haster   …Move on.

Catch   I've meat to offer.
…
You'll not let a man rest his bones?

Haster   I'll have your bones out you don't move away-

The Woman   Let him stay.
…
You don't own the hill.

Haster   …

Haster *settles at the fire, his back to* **Catch**.
Catch *sits and takes some meat from his pack.*

Catch   I'm grateful to you.
You're headed south?

The Woman   Yes.

Haster   You'll not tell our business.

The Woman   I'll tell *my* business to who I care to.

Haster   …

Catch   Your daughter's got fire in her.

The Woman   I'm not his daughter.

Catch   I saw your hands bound-

The Woman   So you think I'm his daughter?

Pause.

Catch There's a lot of sickness down that way.
People dying in the street.
Might be wise to change your plan.

He spits.

The Woman Have you seen it?

Catch My share.
Black flesh. Rot. Stink.
It took the King's daughter.
No one safe from it.
…
Not even the great Lord Haster.

Pause.

Haster You've mistaken me.

Catch You know who your companion is?

Beat.

The Woman Yes.

Catch When I marked you I had to introduce myself.
I've known your stories since I was a boy, sir.

Pause.

Catch Do you know any of them yourself?

Pause.

The Woman The Village in the Hills.

Catch That's a colourful one.
Not a tale you forget easy.
Innards strung through the trees like ribbon.
Men nailed by their tongues to their burning homes.
Speared heads lining the road like sentinels.
They said you could taste the blood on the air for miles around.

The Woman …Is it true.

Catch Oh, it's true. That and hundreds like it.
Back when he was the most feared knight living.
Before he lived long enough to become…*this*.
…
They say the King has tired of him now.
Won't have him near.
Truth is he's envious.
All a man wants is to become a story. To persist.
Our friend here's carved his name into history deeper than-

Haster You've had your meeting.
Now fuck off.

Pause.

Catch *spits. He starts packing away his few things.*

Catch I'd hoped you could help me.
I'm looking for someone.

The Woman Who?

Catch A woman.
Some strange kind of a woman is what they say.

Beat.

The Woman   …what do they say.

Catch   They say- She's lived longer than the mountains.
Longer than the rivers have run.
They say-
Doesn't matter which way you cut her.
How many pieces you put her into.
She'll come whole again and draw breath.
…
Talk is they found her in a village north of here.
Once her strangeness was known, they put her on a fire to burn.
They say she stepped down and walked free.
Never felt the flames.

The Woman   …I heard different.

Catch *spits.*

Catch   Course it's all shite.
Old stories for old cunts.
But some of these cunts have deep purses.
Deeper even than the King's, who wants her for himself.
Has some idea he can take the strangeness from her.
Make himself the same.

Pause.

Catch   It's shaming to see he sent his most feared knight chasing a children's tale.
…
His *former* most feared knight-

Haster *draws his sword and turns-*
Catch *leaps on him and drives his knife into his side-*

Catch   That's all you can give me?

I've waited my whole life to kill you- This is how it is?

He clambers to his feet and spits.

Catch Don't fear-
I'll tell them it was a fight for the ages.
That you were hate incarnate.
I want to kill the legend, not the old man behind it-

He turns to **The Woman**, *who spits in his eye-*

Catch Ah-
…
We've a long way to go together- You want to start like this?
You-
…

He rubs at his eye more frantically as it begins to burn-

He drops to the ground in pain, the scene around him fading.

9.
Lower Paleolithic Age.
We hear a rhythm being pounded on rock.

Catch *looks up from his writhing as a horn blows-*
We're in a cave, lit by flickering flames.

The Woman *steps into the light and stands before him-*
She wears a headdress of bones.

Catch Oh God-
…
Oh God-

*The **Man** in hides from earlier approaches from behind with a sharpened stone-*

Catch   Oh God-

*He pulls **Catch's** head back to slash his throat-*

The Woman   No!

10.
1993.
A bedroom.
Light is flooding in from the hallway.

Ellen   What's the matter?

Pause.

Brooke   …N-Nothing.

Ellen   You were shouting- Do you know what time it is?

Brooke   No-

Pause.

Ellen   You had a bad dream.

Brooke   I thought I was somewhere else.

Ellen   Well you're here. Fourteen Parklands Drive.
Nothing much going on here this time of night.
(Looking out the window.) …We're the only light on, see?

Brooke   You can go back to bed- I'm sorry-

Ellen It's alright. I'll stay a minute.
Get your bearings back.

Pause.

Ellen You've raced through your library books again.

Brooke Yes.

Ellen You can come with me this time. Pick them out yourself.

Brooke No thank you.

Ellen Well I never know what to get you.

Brooke I don't mind.

Ellen I don't know what someone your age- How old are you?

Brooke …

Ellen You really should leave the house at some point.

Brooke You don't have to worry about me.

Ellen Well I do. I don't have much choice in that anymore.
You won't eat anything. You won't go anywhere-
I don't think you sleep, either- I hear you talking to yourself-
Sadie if you will be difficult-

Brooke You're not my mother.

Ellen …No. I'm not trying to be.

Pause.

Brooke   I'll leave if you want me to-

Ellen   That's not what I said, is it.

Pause.

Ellen   You know, I don't sleep much either.
Not for a long time.

Brooke   …Since your son died.

Pause.

Ellen   …How do you know about that.

Brooke   You have pictures. But you don't talk about him.

Ellen   …Well.
Yes.
…

Brooke   That's why you let me stay here.

Pause.

Ellen   I'm letting you stay because you don't have anywhere else to go.

Brooke   You want-

Ellen   I don't want anything from you, Brooke.
Other than to get some fresh air every now and then.
…
You know you can stay as long as you like.

…
Plenty of space here, someone might as well make use of it.

Pause.

Ellen Do you have them a lot. These dreams.
Or whatever they are.

Brooke *(Nods.)*

Ellen Bad things. That happened to you. Or-

Brooke People find me. When it's dark.

Ellen *(Nods.)* …What was this one.
You say it out loud, it'll fritter away to nothing.

Pause.

Brooke …I was in a box.
Underwater.
They put me in a box underwater.

Ellen Who did?

Brooke A- Soldier.
…
I was in there a long time.
I was drowning. Over and over again.

Ellen Did you get out?

Brooke There was a sword somehow-
…
I used it to break the wood- It was rotten.
I swam to the surface.

…
There was a man there. Young.
He was good to me.
Until he wasn't.
Until I wasn't any use to him anymore.

Pause.

Brooke You wouldn't want me here if you knew what I was.

Ellen And what's that.

Brooke …I'm different from everyone else.

Ellen I'll tell you a secret-
Everyone's different from everyone else.
You seem very sure how I feel about things.
You should ask me, next time.
…
You tell your own story.
And don't let others tell it for you.

11.
1979.
The Woman *is looking through the book.*

Evan 'for she dwells
Down in a deep; Calm, whatsoever storms
May shake the world'.
That's Tennyson.
…
There she is giving Arthur his special sword and everything.

The Woman …Excalibur.

Evan There you go. That's who started all this anyway.

The Woman *closes the book and looks at the cover.*

The Woman Dorothy Waites.

Evan She's the one connected all the paintings and accounts and everything.
Tapestries. Statues.
Traced her all the way back to folk tales.

The Woman Does she still-

Evan *(Shakes head.)* Dead. Ages ago.
That was the last thing she wrote. And they didn't print many copies, so if you could be careful with it-

The Woman Can I keep it?

Evan Wh- No- Not-

He takes it back.

Evan Sorry, but-
This is like my most- Irreplaceable, you know?
…You can come back and look at it.
Whenever you like.
Or you can wait and read my book.
My book about the book. That's what I'm doing now, see, so-

The Woman How does it end.

Evan …How does it-

The Woman What does it say happens to her.

Beat.

Evan She's not real, man. There's no eternal…
She's a symbol. Like a wooden horse. Prometheus.
She's just something people were painting into history as this kind of indicator.
Like how she's depicted tells us the mood of the time. Or the King's standing or whatever. Like a mascot.
…
It's a kind of a game that's been running for centuries. That's what the book proved.
Argued, I should say.

The Woman *nods.*

The Woman   …a game.

Pause.

Evan I get how you feel-
You know.
…
I spend so much time with her sometimes *I* forget.
One of my lecturers- Before I left-
He said I talked like I was in love with her.
Like I'd fallen in love with this painting. This idea.
And sometimes it does feel-
When I'm looking for her, now?
I try and find her in contemporary- You know.
It feels like I'm hunting a missing person sometimes.
Someone lost.
…
And I feel bad no one ever gave her a name.
That's something we all get given, right?

12.
1348.
The hilltop.
Haster *wakes with a start. The fire has burnt down to embers.*

The Woman   …You're still breathing.
…
You were shouting at someone. In your sleep.

Pause.

Haster *struggles to sit up, clutching his wound.*
He looks around suddenly-

The Woman   I sent him away.

Haster   …Where.

The Woman   Away.

Beat.

Haster   You said you had no control-

The Woman   I don't. Mostly.

Haster   …But you've done the same to others.

The Woman   When I was able.
Sometimes I had to.
I'm not like you.

Pause.

Haster   Why stay.
Why wait for me to wake-

The Woman   He wants to steal my light.

Haster   …

The Woman   How does he hope to do it.
Some way that hurts me.

Haster   …I know not what-

The Woman   But you'll take me to him anyway.
Whatever he might do to me-

Haster   He is my king.
I go where I am told.

The Woman   And kill who you are told.
…
No one can take it from me.
Many have tried.

Pause.

The Woman *moves over to him.*
She pushes a finger into his wound.
Haster *grunts and struggles.*

The Woman   You've lost a lot of yourself.
Are you afraid?

Haster   …

The Woman   You sounded as if you were.
…
What did you see? That made you cry out.

Pause.

Haster My first kill.

The Woman Who was it.

Pause.

Haster A boy.
A boy I knew.
…
I was alone as a child.
Without name.
Slept in the woods.
Others chased me for sport.
Beat me.
…
I took a rock.
Put an end to the leader of their pack.

The Woman …He finds you at night.

Haster They all do.

Pause.

The Woman Where did you find your name.

Haster The King. He named me.

The Woman He's like your father.

Haster I am a monster to him.
He cannot meet my eye.
…
A man doesn't let his dog eat at the table.

The Woman People call me monster, too.

Haster They also call you God.

The Woman I don't want to be a god.

Haster Better that than monster.

The Woman I want to be like everyone else.

Haster What hope is there of that.
...
For either of us.

The Woman The village I was at before.
They let me stay.
I liked feeding the horses.
Caring for the children.
They taught me to dance.

Haster And when they discovered you?

The Woman ...

Haster Plenty are willing to be near me as well. Until they learn my name.
...
Better to have no name.
To be forgotten.

The Woman Once I forgot who I was.
I gave up and hid myself away until it all left me.
And I had peace.
But in time it came back to me.
At first I'd hear my own stories and think there were others like how I was.
Then I'd come to realise.
And all of it would return.

And that was worse than any pain before.
Any pain you could ever make a person feel.

Haster   …You have what men have wanted as long as they have lived-

The Woman   I have *nothing*.
…
I am denied myself by others telling me what I am.
What purpose I serve to them.
I have seen more than anyone alive, but know less of myself than a child.

Haster   Through living you must have some knowledge of-

The Woman   Why? You men have walked almost as long as I, and you haven't learned anything.
…
I have no knowing even-
If I ever come to an end.
…
Do any of the stories tell of that?
Or am I denied that too.

Pause.

Haster *is losing more and more blood.*

The Woman *moves closer to him.*

She takes his knife.

A moment.

She cuts her thumb open.

The Woman   Hold on to me.
…
Hold *on* to me.

Haster *takes her wrist.*

She presses her thumb into his wound- It glows.

Haster *roars in pain-*

13.
1994.
Haster *is bleeding out on* **Ellen's** *floor, still clutching* **Brooke's** *wrist.*
A sitcom burbles away on the TV.
Ellen *stands in the doorway holding a mug.*

Pause.

Brooke   Help.

Ellen   …wh- How-

Brooke   I had to bring him here.

Ellen   From- Where- He's bleeding-

Brooke   He needs h/elp-

Ellen   Who is he? How did you get him here? I leave the room for a second-

Brooke   He's hurt-

Ellen   That' s not answering-

Brooke You're a nurse.

Ellen *Retired*. I'm a retired nurse- And that doesn't mean you can bring bleeding men in off the-

Brooke He's my friend.
…
I need you to help me.

Pause.

Ellen *steps closer and peers at* **Haster**.

Ellen What's happened to him?

Brooke Someone attacked him- A knife-

Ellen He needs to go to hospital-

Brooke He can't-

Ellen Why not?

Brooke It won't make sense to you.

Ellen It doesn't- None of this-

Brooke We can't go to hospital.
Please.

Beat.

Ellen *leaves.*

Brooke Ellen-!

Ellen *(From off.)* I'm coming back- Hold your horses-

She reappears with a tool box stuffed with medical supplies, kneeling down next to **Haster**.

Ellen Shift. Let me see-
…
Press very hard, there.
He's lucky.

She starts unpacking her supplies; cleaning the wound.

Ellen Most of this stuff is out of date…

Brooke It doesn't matter.

Ellen …Why is he dressed like this? He got attacked in fancy dress?

Haster *is trying to let go of* **Brooke**-

Brooke Hoo- Holde to me. She helpe thee, fool.

Ellen …Hold this. Here. He needs stitches.

Brooke So you can-

Ellen I'm not stitching a knight closed on my living room floor- I don't have-

Brooke Then he'll die.

Ellen …
(To **Haster**.*)* This will hurt.
Is he listening to me?

Haster *has turned his head to watch the sitcom on TV, incredulous.*

Brooke   He's fine. Do it.
…I mean- Please.

Ellen *begins stitching him closed.*

Ellen   …How do you make a friend like this?
How are you making *any* friends. You barely leave the house.

Brooke   He's from a long time ago.

Ellen   I'll say. He smells.

Brooke   He helped me.

Ellen   How's that.

Brooke   He took me somewhere safe.
…
We helped each other.

Ellen   …How did you get him in here so quickly.

Brooke   I told you-

Ellen   You did not.

Brooke   I told you I'm not like anyone else.

Ellen   …Clearly.

She cleans the site of the wound and dresses it.

Ellen   That's the best I can do, but I can't-

Brooke   She mended thee.

Haster   What thyng is this-

Brooke   It kepe thee heeld, leve it. I sende thee agayn now.

Haster   /No-

Ellen   What are you talking like that f-

The Woman *pulls* **Haster's** *hand from her wrist-*

14.
1348.
They're back on the hilltop, the embers still glowing.
Haster *stands shakily and looks around.*

Pause.

Haster   What was that place.

The Woman   …

Haster   You took me-

The Woman   I don't know where.
…
I told you. I don't have control.

Haster   But you know-

The Woman   I can only see- Pieces of it.

Haster   …

Haster *feels at his side-*
Lifts his shirt to reveal the dressing.

The Woman What is it?

Haster …I am mended.

Pause.

The Woman I won't go south with you.
…
I won't be taken anywhere I don't choose myself.
Anywhere I am to be hurt- I won't let you-

Haster North.
…
We'll go north.
…Should you choose.
…
You'll be safer across the border.

Pause.

The Woman You'll go with me.

Haster …*(Nods.)*
I will get you there. Without harm from others.

The Woman You hate me.

Haster …I have tried hating you.
I am unable.

Pause.

She stands.

The Woman North-

Haster I am in your debt-

The Woman Then you can be kind to me.
You can talk to me about whatever I choose, all the way to wherever it is-

Haster I will give you a gift.
…
Should you choose to keep it.

Pause.

Haster Brooke.
…
It means-
River.
…
It is true to what you are.

15.
1353.
A forest, somewhere in the Highlands. Shafts of sunlight pierce the canopy above.

Mason *is here, his face a bloodied wreck.*
He looks around, terrified.

Pause.

He hears something and turns-

Brooke *emerges from the trees, her longbow poised.*

Brooke What are you doing here?

Mason …

Brooke This is our place, no one's to come here.

Mason I- I-

*We hear **Haster** before he appears, carrying firewood-*

Haster You'll have me do all the labour? Cook your meals, build your fires-

*He sees **Mason** and draws a knife-*

Haster Step back.
Back.

Mason *staggers and falls back, scrambling to his feet.*

Haster This is our land-

Brooke I told him.

Haster What brings you here?

Brooke I asked him.

Haster And what did he tell you.

Mason I- I- I-

Brooke This. Where's your sword?

Haster You know well it is lost- Likely by you-

Brooke   I didn't lose it- You should be more careful with it-

Mason points to Brooke-

Haster   You'll put that down should you want to keep it.

Mason *drops his arm.*
Brooke *has wandered closer.*

Brooke   His clothes are strange.

Haster   Step away.

Brooke   He's hurt-

Haster   Step *away*.
...
Brooke.

Brooke   He's scared-

Haster   As he should be.
(To **Mason**.*)* Down on your knees.

Mason *drops to his knees.*

Brooke   No-

Haster   I'll make it quick.

Brooke   He's lost, he didn't do anything-

Haster   You don't know what he's doing here- He will lead others to us.
Move-

Brooke No.

Haster You want to be found?

Brooke I won't let you kill people without cause-

Mason *starts singing in a high, manic yell-*

> Only a thin veil between us,
> My loved ones so precious and true-
> Only as mist before sunrise,
> I am hidden away from your view-

Beat.

Haster What is this-

Again, louder-

> Often I come with your blessing,
> And strive all your sorrows to share-

Brooke *yanks* **Haster's** *arm behind his back-*

Brooke Run! Run!

Mason *trips and stumbles away.*

After a moment, she releases **Haster**.

Haster Now I'm to hunt him-

Brooke You'll not catch him. Not with your knees.
...
Old man.

Haster …

Brooke Let's go home. It's time to eat.

Haster You'll see how wise a decision you made when he returns-

16.
1999.
Brooke *stands in the hall of Ellen's now-dingy house.*
Sunlight floods in from outside, around the shape of **Alice**.

Alice You didn't hear me knocking? Shouting through the letterbox?
I could see you moving around in here. Why didn't you answer?

Brooke I-

Alice Are you Ellen Harpley? No- You look too young-

Brooke I just live here.

Alice With Miss Harpley?

Brooke Yes.

Alice So where is she?

Brooke …

Alice I'll need to speak with her if I'm to-

Brooke She's gone.

Beat.

Alice Gone. Gone how. Where.

Brooke She's-

Alice Dead?

Brooke ...*(Nods.)*

Pause.

Alice You do know when someone dies you need to tell people. People need to know.
I'm here as part of a possession action, do you know what that is?

Brooke N-

Alice It means the bank is taking back this house.
It means a lot of money is owed.
Isn't the power off? The gas? You didn't think to ask why?
...
Was it like this when she was here?
The windows blocked off- All these books-

Brooke I don't have answers to any of your questions.

Alice Well if you want to prove you have a claim to the house you'll need to find some. For all I know you could be-
Are you a relative? Friend?
How did you come to be living here?
When did she die?

Brooke *(Backing away.)* I'll just leave- I can leave-

Alice No, wait a minute- Hold on- Stop-
Who are you?

Brooke No one- I'm no one-

17.
1360.
Brooke *clambers up into the mouth of a cave.*
She looks down into it- The late sun is only creeping down the first few feet.

Haster *comes into view, struggling.*
Brooke *tries to help him, but he waves her away.*
He throws his stick up into the cave and drags himself up the rest of the way.

Brooke This is it?

Retrieving his stick and standing, **Haster** *tosses a rock down into the cave. They listen to it bounce down.*

Haster It's deep.
Go and see.

Brooke …This is what you made us walk here for?

Haster Hm.

Brooke You dragged yourself this whole way to show me a cave?
You won't even walk with me round the lake anymore.

Pause.

Brooke Well. You've shown me.
Let's go-

Haster No.
…

Go down and look-

Brooke At what? It's getting dark, we have to head back-

Haster We're not going back.

Pause.

Haster You'll live here now.
…
Go down as deep as you can.
Stay hidden.

Pause.

Brooke No-

Haster I'm old. No time left.
You'll stay here.
Wait until this plague or the next finishes them all.
…
Once every man woman and child has rotted away to naught, You can come out.
You'll be safe.

Brooke I won't-

Haster I can't protect you-

Brooke I don't need your protection-

Haster They will find you.

Brooke Who?

Haster *Any*one.

…
Any of them.

Pause.

Brooke I won't stay here.

Haster You will.

Brooke I'm going home. To *our* home.
The home we built together.
People don't live in caves-

Haster Well you are not people.
…
Are you.

Pause.

Haster Did you expect this would last forever?
This playing at being a family?
Serving you your imagined meals each night.
Did you not see time cutting at me?
…
I have done you more harm than any of them-

Brooke You gave me my name-

Haster And what good will it serve you?
What good is pretending you're something other than what you are?

Pause.

Brooke Where will you go?

Haster   …While I've my strength-
Tear the hut down-

Brooke   Our *home-*

Haster   Walk into the lake.

Pause.

Haster   You will forget me.

Brooke   I won't.

Haster   In time you will.

Brooke   Never.
…
Even if everything else is stolen from me, I'll remember you.
Always.
I'll chain you to my thoughts and drag you through time.
…
And I will never stay here.
I'll find others-
I'll find others to be with-

Haster   And they will hate you. Over and again.
Or else die and leave you, just as I do now.
Let me leave knowing you will spare yourself the pain.

Brooke   I won't be your redemption.
You're the same as the rest- Wanting me to heal you-

Haster   There is no healing me.

Brooke   As soon as you're gone, I'll leave.

Haster   You'll find sense.

Brooke   I'll *run*.
I'll run as fast as I can-

Haster   Then *go*.
Go back to be burnt.
Drowned.
To be cleaved open and peered at.
There is no home for you.
There can never be.

Brooke   You're my home-

Haster   I wish I'd never laid eyes on you.

Brooke   That's not true-

Haster   You have brought me nothing but confusion-
I ought to hack you to pieces and throw you down there-
Seal it up.

Brooke   I love you-

Haster *advances on her darkly-*

Haster   Don't ever say that.
…
To anyone.
…
I am *death*.
I have killed more than any could number.
I am monstrous-

The Woman   You are *nothing*.

The Woman *glows with a furious rage, terrifying-*
Haster *falls backwards, retreating-*

The Woman   A *smear* of flesh.
I am *all*.
Your armies are *ants* before me.
I will show you what death is-
I will lay waste to *everything*.
I will raze this earth with a fire undying-
I will splinter every soul into pieces, to scatter through time in unending pain.
I will be everything they say I am and more-
And I'll make you watch.
I will leave nothing but the two of us and *dust*.

She calms, her light fading.

The Woman   …I'll show you how I hate them.
How I'm just like you.

Pause.

Haster   We both know you are not.

Pause.

Haster *struggles to his feet.*

The Woman   I won't stay here.

Haster   …Then you'll come back.
…
The youth in your voice will sour,
and you'll come back.
…
…

Goodbye, Woman.

Haster *leaves.*

18.
1998.
Brooke *and* **Ellen** *are walking on the beach together.*
The low afternoon sun shimmers on the waves as they wash onto the sand.

Ellen He used to make me bring him here every weekend.
One Christmas he asked for a metal detector, so then every Sunday we'd be here looking for treasure.
Never found much, of course.
I think his best find was someone's keys they'd dropped walking the dog.
They gave him a fiver as reward.
I think we spotted those without the detector, to be honest.
…
We met a few others doing it once- Older.
He thought they'd want to talk about Roman coins and the like, but they were mostly just interested in finding bits of lost jewellery to sell.
People can be disappointing sometimes.

Ellen *has stopped-*

Ellen …What was I talking about?
…
My head's a sieve these days, I can't even-

Brooke Coming here. Looking for treasure.

Beat.

Ellen Oh.

…
Yes.
…
…
Now he's under the ground himself.

Pause.

Brooke What did that feel like?

Pause.

Ellen It was very-
Unusual.
That's a daft thing to-
…
I couldn't imagine it.
What he'd felt-
It was strange. Trying to think about something I couldn't imagine.
…
I stopped sleeping.
I'd watch the sun come up every morning and think-
'There's been a mistake'. You know-
'The sun can't keep coming up when this has happened'.
'Someone should tell someone'.
How strange.
…
I really didn't do anything much for a very long time.

Pause.

Brooke How did you keep going?

Ellen …Well. You just do, don't you.
…

I didn't want to live my life as one long dying.
I started to try my best to think differently about things.
It took a bit of time, but eventually-
I'd think-
That-
The joy of knowing him was greater than the pain of losing him.
That I was lucky, in some ways.
That I'd had someone to feel sad to lose.
Lots of people don't have that.
…
I'd think how the past is still here in all sorts of ways.
It's not gone, really- It's just-
Taken a different shape.
…
I'd think-
There's always chance-
For something new.

Pause.

Ellen Look at us-!
Who'd have thought I'd meet you?
Who'd have thought you'd ever leave the house?

Pause.

Ellen Come on, let's go home-

Brooke *kisses her.*

Beat.

Ellen What was that for?
What's got into you?
…What's-

The sound of the waves has stopped.

Brooke *walks across to* **Evan**-

We're in his flat in **1979**.
Evan *is rolling a joint whilst* **The Woman** *reads the book.*

Ellen *stares at her son, awestruck.*

Evan Like I said man, studying this stuff doesn't get you fame and glory- It gets you a damp room with a sink to piss in. Not that fame and glory is why we're historians of course, but- Like- A *bit* of glory would be nice. It's mostly a pretty thankless task. Case in point- I found this one book written by a guy who was an air raid warden- Self-published, you know- And in it, he tells this story where he finds a woman in a bomb site with two broken legs. In pain, obviously.
But when he goes to help her, her legs just- Click! Snap back into place, and she runs off. So I thought, nice, someone keeping the torch burning, another enthusiast.
So I track the guy down to a care home and he tries to convince me it's *true*- Says he's never read the Waites book. Says no one ever believed him, but he knows what he saw- And on top of *that* he starts telling me he saw a ghost as well, a knight in armour wandering about-
And I was trying to be polite and all, but I guess he'd gone senile, or-
…What?

Evan *notices* **The Woman** *staring at* **Ellen**, *stood behind him.*

Pause.

He turns to see what she's looking at-

The scene vanishes.

The Woman *is left alone.*

19.

The Woman Alone,
I waited.

Whilst land and water were at war, I watched-
As mountains swept the earth in rolling tides,
The ground beneath my feet a churning mire.

And I walked alone.
And waited.

Through an age of smoke and fog.
Through the supremacy of plants.
Through crowds of beasts indifferent to me,
Who dragged themselves ashore to claim what life
They could before the rains of fire and stone
Cut short their time and drove them into dust.

Until at last I found-
I saw-
Emerging from the trees-
Their spines straightening-
Eyes lifting…
…Here.

I watched them learn.
And love.
And take delight in their young.
And dance…
I watched them choose to move themselves in rhythm with their hearts.
With the hearts of others-
Beating.
On and on.
As they pushed their breath onto the embers of a new era-

And marked me separate from themselves.

Set me apart.

Crowned me some exalted other as they
Clothed me in the tales they told, to thrust me
In a role I'd never sought to play, and
Split themselves along imagined lines to
Spill their blood as though their streams were endless,

And oftentimes I'd grow so tired I'd make
Myself forget. I'd hide myself away
And close my eyes in pantomime of sleep,
Waiting. As time stole all I knew from me.
But back each happening came against my will,
Fast rising in my throat like jagged stones,
To tell me once again I am alone.

And so I broke.

And returned. To a place from long ago-
A cave. Once claimed for me by one I'd known-
A friend.

And I descend, in hope I'd find some trace
Of him remained, to sit hidden from light,
And let the insects make their homes within my flesh-
And feel my skin fuse fast into the rock,
And wish with everything to fall asleep.

And I become a children's tale, a myth.

A footnote in books left unread on shelves.

Until their faith in me renews again.
And brings them all outside my cave to beg.

To keen. To plead deliverance. To pray.

I hear their sorrow drifting down but tell
Myself it's all a dream, a cruel nightmare,
The issue of a weary broken heart.
So conjure up another in its place-
A woman born who lived without event,
And died surrounded by her family,
Stitched tight with all through her impermanence.

And then they're gone.

And I emerge, beneath skies of puce and rust,
To walk across a sea of bones bleached white
As what few living things remain come circling,
Seeking comfort as their faltering hearts
Slow gently to a halt. I sit and watch
The withered trees and plants retreating fast,
The final structures tumbling into ash,
Then climb upon the tallest peak to see
The sun colossal, drawing nearer still,
Seducing stone to ecstasies of fracture
As everything below diminishes
Through immolation, losing shape and sense
As gases flare and burst up through the ground
In colours never visible before-
The bacchanal above in harmony,
A boiling tumult hurling tendrils out
To wrap my form and coax my feet to leave
The roiling earth below and form the new
Axis amongst the stars, as from beyond
Race planets, orbits snapped, colliding with
Their many-numbered moons with thunderous force-
The stars in their quintillions closing in
To veil my shape with bloated swelling forms,
Then bursting in totality, now come

Annihilating orchestras of light-

Until as quick the all shrinks to a point
Of brilliance infinitesimal-

Drifting about the void we're held within.

I reach, and let it sail into my hands.
And know this spark might come to life anew-
Should I choose to ignite it with a breath.

This light and I. Alone. Together.

And I think of her.

And what she told me.

And I cradle the glow.
And wait.
And wonder.

Appendix

All other characters are to be played by the performers playing Mrs Lyall, Mason, and Haster.

Here is the suggested breakdown:
Mrs Lyall – Ellen; Alice
Mason – Aulus; Len; Evan; Catch
Haster – Man (I:5/II:9).

Figure (II:2), Narrator and Academic can be assigned to any of the three.

*

The song that commences the séance is 'Only a Thin Veil Between Us' by C. Payson Longley. It was written after 1863, but I think you can give me a break.
I am thankful to Matt Marble and his music preservation website Secret Sound Project (mattmarble.net/secret-sound) for providing me with the sheet music.

*

Thanks to Rory Mullarkey for his translations and support throughout the writing.

I am grateful to the books *The Darkened Room* by Alex Owen and *The Table Rappers* by Ronald Pearsall for guiding me through the world of Victorian spiritualism; and of course *The Woman in Time* by Dorothy Waites for providing much of the play's central conceit.

all
of
it

to be spoken aloud by one performer,
quickly

all of it was first performed at the Royal Court Jerwood Theatre Downstairs, Sloane Square, on Friday 7 February 2020, with the following cast and creative team:

Kate O'Flynn

Director Vicky Featherstone
Lighting Designer Anna Watson
Assistant Director Izzy Rabey

Rushing
Rushing
Rushing
Rushing
Rushing
Press
Bright
BrightbrightbrightBIG
More
More More In
In
InInInIn
More
InIn
Fill
FillFullFill
Close
Closer
Down
Shhhhhhh

Face
Faces
Face
Colour
Bright
Brightbrightbright
In
In
In
InInIn
Face
Faces
Close
Down
Shhh
Up
Down
Shhh
Up
Down
Shhh
Down
Loud Louder

Soft
Hard
Down
Bright
No
No
No
No
No
Yes!
Feet
Feet there
There That
Feet Foot

Feet
Face

        Wet
        Wet
       Water
         In
         In
         In
        Out
        No
   Nonononono
         A
        Ah
        Ow
       Shh
       Kiss
       Kiss
       Face
       Kiss
 Fill Full Fill
      Down
      Down
  Shhhhhhhh

                         Ta Ta Ta Ta Ta Ta
                         BBBBBBBBBB
                                 Face
                                Faces
                                Smile
                               Smiling
                                    Yes
                                    Yes
                              Yes Yes Yes
                               bbbbbbbb
                                 Speak:
                                   RED
                                   Yes!

redredredredredredredredredredredredredredredredredred
       Dog is red
       Door is red
       Floor is red
       red red red
        Red
        Red
        Red
        Red
        Red
        Red
        Red
        Red
        Shhh
        Red
        Red
        Red
        Red
        Red
       Fill Full Fill
        In
       Down

Rrrrr
Red
Face
Mmmmm
Mum
Ma
Ma
Mummy
Ma
Mum
Face
Face
Shhh
Down
Down

MUM
Yes!

     Step
     Yes
     Step
     Yes
     Yes
    YesYesYes
     Step
     Over
     Oops
   OopsOopsOops
     Oops
     Shhhh
     Shh
     Oops
     Down

          MUM
          RED
          DOG
          DA
          DAG
          DOD
MURRMURRMURRMURRMURRMURRMURR
          In
          In
         Food
          FOO
        FOOFOOFOO
          In
         Shhh

     Meow
     Moo
     Woof
     Baaa
     Tweet
   Tweet Tweet Tweet

Bad
No
Bad
Not
No
Not not not No
No
No
NoNoNo
Bad
Shhh
Shh
Down

                        Bad
                        Bad
                        Bad
                        Bad
                 (badbadbadbad)

                                          Where's?
                                          There's!
                                          There
                                          Face
                                      MUMMY
                                          Face
                                            DA
                                            DA
                                            DA
                                            DA

                        Hands
                        Hands
                        Hands
                        Hands
                        Hands
                        Hands
                        Hands
                        Hands

Oops
Oops
Oops
Kiss
Kisses
Face
Faces
MA
MA MA MA
Oops
Sore
Sore bit
Sore
Kiss
Kisses
(redredredred)

Boy
Girl
Man
Woman
Dog
Cat
Mouse
Tree
Sky
Grass
Green
Blue
Red
RED
Car
Cars
Tractor
Tractor
123
Onetwothree
12345

                                              Bird
                                              Birds
                                              House
                                      Mummy Daddy
                                              House
                                                Dog
                                               Dogs
                                                Hot
                                               Cold
                                               Oops
                                               Oops
                                                 Yes

                        Good Yes
                         Bad No
                        Good Yes
                         Bad No
                           No
                           No
                           No
                           No
                           No
                            NO
                          NONONO
                       NONONONONO

Chick-en
Chick-en
There's you
There's me there's you
There's daddy there's me there's you
There's mummy
There's
Over there
There
House
                              Out
                              Out
                              Wee

Wee-Wee
There
Over there
There's there
In there
Wee-Wee
ppp
Poo
In there
Over there

Who's there
(dogs go-)
Woof
Dog
food there is dog food and people food and cat food (there is a cat in that house)
And the sky
And the sky
And the sky
And the sky
And the stars at night
And the sun in the day
And the stars at night
And the moon
And

when the big hand and the small hand THREE
I'll come
She'll come
They'll come to get
get me
Lunchbox
Sandwiches in my lunchbox
There is peanut butter in the sandwiches
In the sandwiches in the lunchbox in my

3

Name my name
My name is
Hello my name is

Hello
Mrs Smith
Good morning
Good (yes) morning
Hello my name is
My name is (mummydaddyme)
My name is
Helen Deborah Amy Sarah
Simon Eric Edward Joe Jack
Boys
Girls
Mrs Smith
There
I like don't like
Home hometime Big hand small hand home house mummy daddy me
(bighandsmallhand)

Numbers
Words
Over there
In
I like I don't like
Look like me
Look different (different)
Tuppence Vagina
Vagina
Vagina
In there
In my lunchbox there are
Boys at my table
Boys There are Boys
There are
Willy
Penis
Vagina Vagina Vagina
V V V
The names
Are different

Look different
Mr Casey (boyspenis)
Good morning Good Morning Mr Casey Good morning
My pencil case has
My pencil case has you can smell this one red (red) smells like strawberry
Blue blueberry brown chocolate yellow lemon
Lemon lemon lemon
Lemon is my favourite colour
My mummy says I'm getting a little brother Helen has a little brother
Amy has a bigger brother I have no brother I'm
getting a little brother (my pencil case has)
Smaller than me
Smaller than me I can hold
I can be careful I'm careful Careful
I'm bigger big bigger bigger sister I'm the biggest sister I have a little
brother I can be
Responsible
Responsible
Responsible Grown up I can be Grown Up I have to be
Grown Up now (in my pencil case)
My little brother (boyspenis) David
Balls
Balls
(the testes)
small smaller smallest hands are in my hands These are my hands
These are his hands and I'm
not allowed to watch tv too much it gives you square eyes that's not
true Eric says that's not true that's just what Grown Ups say they lie
like how they lie about everything like how they lie about Santa like
how they lie about
Santa
Santa is real but Mummy and Daddy help him he has so many
houses true
Not true
Kids stuff
Kids
Grown ups Grown Grown

grown ups
Keep it nice
Make it nice for David don't tell
Secrets
Lies
Nice lies
Secrets/Lies Secrets are nice lies and

Some things are
Easier than other things and some things there are things
And things and things
And here's where we are and this is England and this is Britain and
this is Europe and this is America
That's
America Australia Kangaroos kangaRoos upside
Down Paris French Bonjour
There are other things
And other water
There is water
Seas
Oceans
Boats
Planes
Over there
Me mummy daddy david there are other

Joe's grandad died
Joe is sad
Dead Death
Heaven
Heaven?
(Hell)
There is a good place and a bad place
There are other things and other places and
(americaaustraliakangaroo) you can't
To some
I have two grandads and one grandma
I have
Everyone
Everyone dies

Everyone dies
Everyone dies
One day
Not today
Or tomorrow
A long time
A long long way away
Mum says
Everyone (mummydaddydavidme) dies
Everyone dies
Everyone dies
Go and play
Everyone dies
Don't think about it
(everyonedies)
everyonedieseveryonedieseveryonedies
I have a new coat
(everyonedies)
My new coat is green
(everyonedies)
It has pockets
It has zips
I have a new coat
My new coat isveryonedies
This is important there are things that are importantvryonedies and you have to work hard and if you work hard thendies you will have a better life there are people with sad livesvryone dies who didn't work hard and if you want to have a nice life you have to work hard

Test
Testing
Test (testicles)
This is important there are things that are important Maths
I'm not good at maths
Maths
[   ]
I can't
Can't
(important)

Work hard and you'll do well People who work hard do well
Can't
Can't
Can't
Can't
(everyone dies)
Can't
Can't
Can't Can't Can't Won't Don't

like
Dolls
Girls girly girl things
Horses
Horses bite horses can bite you (everyone dies)
Beans
Broccoli
Vegetables?

I like
Robots
Space
Dinosaursvryonedies
(Extinct)
stories books stories I like stories
(lies/secrets/lies)
There are things-
Ice cream

Ice
cream hurts
Ow
OW
My new coat is
Ice cream for holidays
Coke is for holidays
I like coke
Coke is bad for your teeth David isn't allowed coke I'm allowed coke
I'm a grown up responsible girl Woman I'm a Woman Call her a
woman if she wants to be called a woman I think it's sweet
Grown Up

Other families go to america Disney other families go to spain
it's sunny in spain there are places where it's sunny all the time
it's not sunny in the lake district it's wet it rains I like rain
there is water here there is water on the water
Some things you like sometimes some things you like all the times
Holidays
Summer holidays are long longer
Your mother has to work
Your mother has to work sometimes
Sometimes it's just us
(medaddydavid)
After the holidays
I have new shoes
After the holidays you have to
After the holidays you have to go back to

Big school big shoes big bag big books carried onto big bus they told
us
year sevens get
Babies get
Year Sevens get pushed around
I used to be big
I used to be the biggest
We
Me and Helen eat our lunch Amy doesn't-
Everyone here smells different There are too many smells here
Everyone smells like their house Every house has a smell Your house
has a smell but you can't smell it
Died Dead Died My Grandad Died No I Didn't Go To The Funeral
(everyonedies) at funerals there are dead people there are dead and
We're not friends anymore
They're not friends anymore so we can't be friends anymore
You can lose friends and you don't get them back
They're not friends anymore because
Boys
Because of boys
There is a boy
They kissed

*It's not called kissing no one calls it kissing they got off with each
other it's called
being square are you square
I don't know
If you've never kissed anyone you're square
I did kiss someone but it was on holiday so you wouldn't know them
They're not friends anymore
You can lose friends and not
don't want to be square I think I want to not be square the most in the
world* SEX
the most I ever wanted anything is to not be square SEX
I want to not be square please god SEX
Please I don't want to be SEX
*It's wet and our teeth are clinking together it hurts he's licking my
filling (can you lick a filling out?) I don't want a boyfriend I just
want to be friends
I don't want to be friends with anyone ever like that*
-SIMON TYLER IS MY FIRST KISS-
*I can hear myself saying how I liked it I can hear myself saying
things I don't
think I say things I don't think
a lot all the time*

*I've never done that
Down there
Masturbate
There's a name for It by the way
It's a video everyone has to watch, it's old The Women have full
bushes women don't have bushes anymore
They don't?
Do I have a bush
Not like that
I've never done that
In the bath in bed in the wendy house in the garden on the sofa
behind the sofa in the cupboard I've never done that
everywhere all the time
If you do it for a long time it produces a pleasurable sensation called
an orgasm
Stop having Orgasms*

Don't have an Orgasm
Oh you love it so much I bet you're having Orgasms
I never did that In the bath in bed in the wendy house in the garden
behind the sofa in the cupboard under the stairs I've never done it
long enough to get the
(pleasurable sensation called an orgasm)
Oh
Oh
I'm going to break it
I'm going to break myself somehow
(everyonedies)
why can't we have cubicles cubicles to change changing body
your bodies are changing mine isn't changing enough it's broken
I broke it broken blood I'm broken feel broken blood blood bleed
Woman WOMAN ♪ girl you'll be a woman ♪
Why are you crying it's not a big
biggest in school is what they
Big is better because
(pleasurable sensation called an orgasm)
I thought the clitoris
(pleasurable sensation called an orgasm)
But that's not proper Proper SEX WITH BOYS
WITH BOYS
BOYS
PENISES
Everyone has a penis all boys have penises
they're hiding they're just hiding them
(Simon Tyler)
Just hiding them like they're
(Hard-ons)
Did Simon Tyler
(the penis fills with blood causing it to become erect)
Did Simon Tyler get a hard-on
You're giving him a hard-on
Boner
Boners
He's got a boner They've got a boner Got a boner in art Get boners
all the time

> *Bonersbonersboners*
> *There are boners*
> *Everywhere*
> *There are boners everywhere I'm surrounded by boners*
> *gaygaygaylesbianslesbianslesbosdykeslezzaslezzaslezzlezzlezzlet you*
> *let you if you ask*

At Jenna's party you're invited
I'm invited to Jenna's party
I have to wear
I hope when I get home my wardrobe has all new clothes in
I hope when I get home all my old clothes have burnt
Jenna's party
I hope when I
Be careful
We're trusting you
No one else's parents have ever been this scared of a party in the history of all parents
Big house
Dad be cool
I'm cool
No you're not
Pick you up at eleven but call if you want to leave sooner
I think I'm going to want to stay forever I think parties are meant to last until the dawn I saw on tv once

THERE IS ALCOHOL AT THIS PARTY

> *Everyone's drunk*
> *Not yet don't be stupid*
> *It takes time to get drunk*
> *At christmas I see my mum drunk*
> *You can get too drunk*
> *You can become an alcoholic*
> *Not from one party don't be stupid*
> *Beer is for boys*
> *The blue one drink the blue one*
> *Pretend you have it all the time*
> *It's very*

[

                ?

                              ]

disappointed in you
trusted you
Your father couldn't come to bed until gone one it took so long to clean the car
Who knows what you did
In a state like that who knows who did what to you
Boys at your age and older
Older boys
Prey
(I'm Prey Girls are Prey) RAPE RAPE
I'm going to buy you an alarm And spray
I don't think the spray is legal
You can buy spray Spray is a thing girls are allowed because of
Boys and their
Penises
Don't talk like that in front of your brother
                Jenna's party
            I was at Jenna's party
         I was so wasted at Jenna's party
       I really don't remember I was so Wasted
        I was so Wasted at Jenna's party
          Got Wasted *at Jenna's party*
              Is it true you
          Got Wasted *at Jenna's party*
              Is it true you
            Got Wis it true you

                            Just ask I bet
                  Just ask and pretend you're wasted
                    (got Wasted at jenna's party)
                        just ask to see it
                            They'll show
                            They want to
                        They want to show

They want us to see
I saw
I saw
At a party
Lots of parties
I've been to lots of parties
I'm the kind of person that goes to parties
And sees
He showed
We saw
Laughed
Don't laugh
Not because
But
Hair everywhere
So many (pubes)
And Doesn't seem that
Wasn't even
Hard-on
If you want to
No thanks
I have seen two penises (four but two don't count)
I have seen two penises I have kissed one boy I think
none of my friends like me
I think the inside of my head is different to the inside of their heads
I think I am different
I think I have no friends even though I say I do
I think people pretend a lot
I think I am pretending all the time
It feels like wood inside a sock but skin
A skin sock
(why they call it a woody sometimes)
I don't feel any different but on the way home I kept my hand in
my pocket the whole time in case my mum could see is that weird?
No I get that
I think Jessica is my best friend
I think Jessica is the only real person in the world

I don't want to do tongues thanks
That's what kissing is
I just think
Just go with it, Jesus
There are wars on tv there are people being blown up like in films on
tv on tv they
say

People say
I'm a slut
So what they can say what they want
I don't want to be a SLUT *though*
I think sluts can make them CUM
Shut up I did my best
Hahaha
Girls who have sex are sluts and boys who have sex are just boys I
think
things are very different all over and no one acts like they are at all
Every film I see has naked boobs but you never see a willy
Jessica's tits TITS *are bigger than mine*
My bum is bigger than Jessica's
Jessica thinks Holden Caulfield is the fittest boy in the world but I
think he seems hard work
I like loud music and sad music
I don't like the words pussy or cunt
Some people are artists There are artists who aren't painters
Art is not just painting
Kurt Cobain killed himself
I don't think I believe in God
I don't believe in God
My parents don't believe in God
I think my Mum does not believe in God I don't know about Dad
I don't know what David believes
I don't believe in Heaven or Hell
I wonder if God is something everyone grows out of
No because look at priests
And there are muslims And there are buddhists and there are jews and
I am not anything and I don't believe in God
I have never been on a plane

Do you feel different?
Not really
Does it hurt
It's sore yeah
How sore
Like a thing is going in where there wasn't a thing going in before
And it was okay it doesn't feel
I didn't have a . . .
(pleasurable sensation called an orgasmcum CUM CUM)
Like a thing is going in where there wasn't a thing going in before
Square peg round hole
It hurts but not so much He
wore a johnny (condom) that was flavoured but I didn't put it in my mouth
You're not a virgin anymore
No
But it doesn't Feel feels like
Judy Blume lied to me
Like a thing is going in where there wasn't a thing going in before
Maybe it's different in America
Dave Barnsley
DAVID BARNSLEY
SEX
I am Having Sex with David Barnsley
I am being Fingered by David Barnsley
I wish my first time was with someone with a different name from my brother
I wish there was a better word than Fingered
I don't think Meg Ryan gets Fingered
fingers are spiky
SEX
I don't want to be on top and I want the lights off
David Barnsley is okay
David Barnsley has not been reported to have the biggest in school
but it comes out the top of my fist when I hold it
He tells me he's worried he'll cum straight away
His breath smells like pasta sauce
Everyone smells like their house

My eyes are used to the dark so I can see the ceiling
The ceiling in his parents' bedroom has wallpaper on it,
how do you wallpaper a ceiling?
Like a thing is going in where there wasn't a thing going in before
Some people do it in the bum
I guess you have special ladders
You're doing well in everything except maths
I hate maths
I will never have to do maths again, no more maths I will
carry a calculator everywhere so I never have to do maths
And some people go to Cambridge And some people go to Oxford
That's another thing
You have to do special
I think some people are classist
Classist
I think some people are Classist
Yes, we know you learnt a new word sweetheart
Racist Classist Homophobe Homophobic
I think you're Homophobic, Dad
I think some of the things they say are wrong I think they're wrong
I think I'll put Newcastle as my second choice
Jessica is going to a different university
If I go here and you go here that's different sides of the country
We can phone and email And message
And my mum says trains are not so expensive
We can visit
I think I'll never meet anyone more perfect than you
I think if I could I'd let you walk around
in my body and I wouldn't be worried
When my parents look at me can they see I've had David Barnsley's penis inside me
twice
Does it show in how you walk
I think when I asked Dan to stop kissing me he should have
I will never pass my exams and I'll be homeless and die Alone
I don't need a cake you don't have a cake for your eighteenth
I had a cake for my eighteenth
Yeah like a hundred years ago

Alright
They'd probably just invented cake cake had only just come out
Okay thank you
    You're allowed more than one friend to stay if you like you know
    Three B's and a C in General Studies
    no one cares about General Studies (poor mrs hall)
    I'm going to university which is what you're meant to do
    Are you sure you don't want to take it
    No
    I think you'll miss it when you get there
    I don't need it

    I am leaving home
    I am moving away
    This is what people do
    I'll be back
    For christmas for holidays for weekends if I like
    I'm "Leaving Home"
I have a new room with a sink in it a bedroom with a sink in it the shower is down the hall it's shared shared shower and this is the number for security and this is your key for your room and your key for the block as a whole there's no lift I'm afraid your parents can park up just here to help you unpack but there's a two hour maximum period you can stay

    I have to
    stay
    here
    Call us at the weekend so we know how you're getting on
    We won't hug you in front of everyone (please do please hug me please don't let me go evereverevereverever)
    Ever need any just let me know I already have a guy I think when it's fresher's week they just walk up and down giving out their number
    A drug dealer *a* drug dealer's
    DRUGS
    Most of them are just
Act like you do this all the time even though it feels like your head is filling up with some kind of something metal I never met a girl stoner before

Is this you?
Yeah
You still had to wear uniform at sixth form
It was a fancy school
I think my family were probably poor
Most people here are not poor
Most people here are not from the north
Most people here seem like they've already been here for years
I have never had a conversation with someone who wasn't white
Some parts of the country are all white and some are not and
Am I a racist by accident
Do I not have to go in every day?
What am I meant to do the whole time?

I want to be a poet
Don't say that it sounds stupid don't say that
I write poetry
I write poetry sometimes
Sometimes I like to write poetry
Sometimes
The parties here smell different to how parties used to smell
(don't just stand in the corner at least look like you're waiting for someone to get back they'll be back any second i'm just waiting)
Eventually your friends there will be just
as good as the friends you had at school
I only had one friend at school
So then you'll have new friends who are as close as Jessica
Has already got a boyfriend I should have a boyfriend
You'd like him he's into film
("into film")
He's Into Film and he reads a lot
Yeah I have lots of friends here too it's all really cool and I'm writing lots of poems
You should come and visit
Oh yeah I will just when I'm not so busy maybe there's all- There's so much-

Your mother is very ill

Your mother is very ill and she's not going to get better

Isn't it a nice room they gave me
(no no no it's not no)

You'll have to all stick together Be kind to each other
Look after your brother

It's raining

why did it have to rain today

this is something that happens to other people

Of course you're going back
No-
She wouldn't want you to miss any more She hated a fuss
Yes-
You have to finish your degree
Yes
You can tell them, the university, they'll make allowances There'll be a procedure
yes

This really isn't good enough, can you talk me through what happened here
What happened is fuck you what's the point just pass me pass pass pass me so I can tell my dad I passed I don't need to know about Chaucer no one needs to know about Chaucer not ever Chaucer is not anything anyone needs to know about ever in the world ever

Dad says you're not doing well at school
I'm fine
Dad says-
You don't have to give me the big sister talk
I know-
I'm fine
Yes

Are you okay?

Yes
Just you're sort of- Wasted
A lot

I'm fine
Everything's fine everything has always been fine fine is the word I
would apply to all of this I have to retake a year but so what anyway
it's not like it even matters
Why do you care anyway
Because we're

                              friends

Friends
Friends
This is like a sitcom They could make a sitcom about the three of us living together and people would watch it and think I wish I could live with those girls in that flat
(Your brother's in trouble again)
>*Our parties are the best because it's exactly the right amount of people people who come the right amount of people people who come who came (i don't like to bother you with it Tell Me Tell Me Always Tell Me) he*
>>*he*

HeHeHeHeHeHe is talking to me with that shy smile that I don't think he knows he does
>*he like me as much as I*

like a film They could make a film about the two of us living together and people would watch it and think I wish I had what they had Hands Lips Eyes your brother's in trouble again Looking at Me My brother David, this is Max Max this is my Dad nice to meet you nice to meet you a FilmMaker gosh Steven Spielberg Our house is too small everything here is tiny I don't think it's
people sized And no I don't want to have sex in my childhood bedroom thanks very much and last time
cystitis cystitis cystitis cystitis would
She like him as much as I like him not the same but see how he makes me please keep it short dad
Oh don't worry it'll feel short because of all the great jokes I'll be telling
And obviously the one person who we wish was here
Is this the most obvious song we could have picked has this wedding happened ten thousand thousand times- why have I worn these pants I am so uncomfortable and there's no way I'll even want to by the time we get back to-
I like reading the guidebook because it tells me where to look I don't know otherwise
Yes we had a wonderful time
I didn't want to call and spoil your honeymoon but I'm afraid your brother's-

You can't keep doing things like this
It was nothing
You went to Jail
For a few weeks it's not
It doesn't matter how long
I'm fine (fine) *you live your life and I'll live mine how*
Why would they ask where you'll be in five years when obviously
everyone thinks hopefully not still here I hope I'll be exploring
avenues in management and overseeing my own projects and
A BABY
A BABY WILL BE COMING OUT OF ME
IN NINE MONTHS A BABY WILL COME OUT OF ME
You said you were going to paint the room
It doesn't matter what colour it is, she won't notice
I don't think it's sunk in I don't think it'll ever sink in I think
I'm the first woman in the world to not entirely realise a
BABY IS COMING OUT OF ME
I'M GOING TO BREAK SOMETHING SOMETHING'S
WRONG SOMETHING'S WRONG MY SPINE
IS GOING TO
Oh

you're looking right at me

i think i was expecting a thing but you're a person aren't you

I'm just saying it's very good timing you read that article as it means
I'm the one that has to get up to do All The Feeding
Your brother has a job and is doing really well
I don't have a mother I am a mother and I don't have a mother
I need an adult I need a grown up
My nipples feel like they need replacing

*My dad is a grandad my dad is old my dad somehow looks smaller
than the baby when he's holding the baby the baby is my baby that's
my daughtereveryonedies I have a daughter Don't drop her
Don't throw her
Don't step on her
Don't sit on her
Don't poison her
Don't choke her
Don't set her alight
Don't electrocute her
Don't drown her
Don't cut her into bits no
No I want you to keep working on your film I'm too tired to do much
else than sit with her anyway you're very talented don't say that keep
 going you need to use this time because once I'm back at work
Back at work
Back at work
Back in this car at this time of day with this radio I don't even like
this show why do I listen to this every day driving to work
Driving to work
Driving to work
Driving to work
Driving to work
Driving to work
Driving to work
Driving to work
Driving to work
Driving to work
Driving to work
Driving to work
Driving to work
Driving to work
Driving to work
Driving to work
Driving to work
Driving to work
Driving to work
 That's called Motor Skill and she's meant to be better at it by now
 So she's clumsy she's our lovely clumsy girl*

Driving to work
Driving to work
Driving to work
Driving to work
Driving to work
Driving to work
Driving to work
Driving to work
Driving to work
Driving to work
Driving to work
Driving to work
Driving to work
Driving to work
Driving to work
Driving to work
Driving to work

> *I always thought we'd have three*
> *We can barely manage with one*

Driving to work

> *The cost of childcare is obscene actually obscene*

Driving to work
Driving to work
Driving to work
Driving to work
Driving to work
Driving to work
Driving to work
Driving to work
Driving to work
Driving to work
Driving to work
Driving to work
Driving to work
Driving to work
Driving to work

Your father and I just think-
He doesn't think anything, it's you it's all just you
and what you think

Driving to work
Driving to work
Driving to work
Driving to work
Driving to work
Driving to work
Driving to work
Driving to work
Driving to work
Driving to work
Driving to work
Driving to work
Driving to work
Driving to work
Driving to work
Driving to work

You have to be reasonably realistic with what
grades you're going to get
You said I can go wherever I want
You can but you have to-

Driving to work
Driving to work
Driving to work
Driving to work
Driving to work
Driving to work
Driving to work
Driving to work
Driving to work

Are you sure you don't want to take it
No
I think you'll miss it when you get there
I don't need it

Driving to work
Driving to work
Driving to work
     Call us once a week that's all we want
        Okay-
        I love you
       Mum please-

Driving to work
Driving to work
Driving to work
Driving to work
Driving to work
Driving to work
Driving to work
Driving to work
Driving to work
Driving to work
Driving to work
Driving to work I have to leave my brother has died

  He was doing really well but I don't know something just
        (look after your brother)

        (look after your brother)

        (look after your brother)

     I'm sorry Mum
     thank you sweetheart

Driving to work

Driving to work

Driving to work
Driving to work
Driving to work
Driving to work
Driving to work
Driving to work
    Well I don't see why you can't just work on it here that's what the spare room's for

Driving to work
Driving to work
Driving to work
Driving to work
Driving to work
Driving to work
Driving to work
Driving to work
Driving to work
Driving to work
Driving to work
Driving to work
Driving to work
Driving to work
    Nothing's happened we just don't particularly want to be married anymore

> *I don't see why I have to tell her-*
> *Because she probably already knows It's extremely fucking obvious*
> *No, he's not a bad person He was very talented when he was younger*
> *He's still talented,*
> *you're right*

Driving to work
Driving to work
Driving to work
Driving to work
Driving to work
Driving to work
Driving to work
Driving to work
Driving to work
Driving to work
Driving to work
Driving to work
Driving to work
Driving to work

> *A poet? God*
> *I don't think I've ever once had a poetic thought*

Driving to work
Driving to work
Driving to work
Driving to work
Driving to work
Driving to work
Driving to work
Driving to work
Driving to work

> *I still have friends If you're close enough with your*
> *friends you don't have to see them*
> *Or call them*

Driving to work
Driving to work
Driving to work
Driving to work

Driving to work
Driving to work
I can't call the post office because they'll ask what it is I'll just buy another They're so expensive though and there's nothing to be ashamed of I'm a grown woman with perfectly normal

Driving to work
Driving to work
Driving to work
Driving to work
Driving to work
Driving to work
Driving to work
Did you make the cake? Oh, it's from Marks?
Am I a terrible person for expecting better cake after thirty-six years of working here Yes yesyes absolutely
So much time now you've got
So much time now
To do all those things you always wanted to do and I don't remember the things I wanted to do and
Retirement's the best kept secret that's what I've always said the best kept secret
So many things to do
To do
That's right
Did you ever consider getting a cat Dad
A cat? No, I'm not a cat person
(Do you blame me for not being able to talk to him I could never talk to him he didn't want to be talked to I didn't try hard enough) and
AND WE'RE GETTING MARRIED
Marriage is a wonderful thing-
You say
I don't regret marrying your father
You think it's too soon
I think it's right if you think it's right he seems very nice tall broad
Sex it must be sex sex can make all sorts of things seem like good ideas her choice her choice I don't I can't

Dad says he's really happy
That's good
He's going to write a speech
Well we're all still waiting for his film
That's mean
It is, I'm sorry
People don't give me leaflets anymore I walk past people promoting
things and they don't see me as a reasonable home for their flyer I am
not a target demographic I don't know when that
happened I never see a woman my age on tv or in a film having a
good time I never see a woman my age I never see women my age
maybe they don't see me either we're all just as invisible to each other
as we are to everyone else
Dress Hat Photos Photos Photos Speech Toast Speech Toast Speech
Toast Sore palms Cake Dance Drunk Drunker Bed
I think he's probably a moron but he's a nice
enough moron I suppose
Your granddad's died but I don't expect you to come back for the
funeral if you're busy
Probably for the best much longer and

Ash

You were the biggest man in the world and now you're just ash *you*
used to step over buildings and I don't know what all this is I see
myself in photographs I see people in photographs and I'm
For the poetry? fewer people here than I supposed there would be
even fewer than I guessed there would
be at a poetry evening at a library in a small town most older than
me here because they've even less than me
to do
this I used to want to do this is this what I wanted to do or did I just
like the
Idea
Poem Poem Poem Poem Poem Applause
There are crumbs under my seat
Poem Poem Poem Applause
Published apparently I suppose I think I could maybe
Yes thank you Yes I used to Yes maybe at the next-
It's weekly It's going to be weekly This is Bill I forget your surname

Teacher Teacher at school new to town English "The Local Scene"
Hahaha
Maybe I'll see you at the next

evening
Everything feels
clammy Everyone can hear my thighs sticking together there is no microphone rooms this small don't need microphones

~POEM~

Do you remember me Oh yes I'm Bill Lowell I teach at The teacher
yes that's right I
Loved Your Poem
Thank you so much I was so nervous
You didn't seem to be
I was so nervous I've never done this even when I was Yes why not I could show you the places to be I could show you some things it's only
a small

Died doesn't say passed away says died she died
I'm sorry yes my brother [   ]
That's very
Late it's very late do you think he has very very very blue bluest eyes and Lips lipslips
can't go in a shop like that there are no women in the photos in the window who look like me I Can't ridiculous

Oh
Oh
OH
Well-
That was-
Yes-

I hardly knew what I was
Want to wear a dress not one of those suits like old Old Ladies wear
Old Old I'm Weddings are for the Young not
No your father's not invited
Because it wouldn't be appropriate
Of course he's family
I would really like you to be there
Of course I do

Dress Photo Speech Toast Applause Cake Dance Bed
Scotland Read Reading
Talking Talking Talking Talking Talking Talking
a valve opened somewhere
Does he love me more or less or just the same as his first wife do I love
him more than my first I feel I love him more than anything or
anyone today
I can't force her to talk to me
She's welcome here whenever she'd like to yes I'm sure your parents
separating but I lost my mother and (look after your) brother and I
didn't stop I don't think I'm
being the stubborn one here
Here
Here she is
Here she is!
Don't cry
Don't cry, I love you, don't cry
It wasn't so long don't cry I forgive you I forgive you I forgive
everything I'm the great forgiver
It's so nice to see you I see you I see you I can see you until you're
back in my arms right back just a speck a tiny speck carrying a tiny
speck speck that's you
due
in June In June she's due in June a summer baby a new baby for the
summer (read somewhere about population absolute crisis point
everyone dies) a grandma me The Grandma I'm Grandma not
granny far too old Grandma please
can I be a Grandma can I be a Grandma's House can I be that
house my grandparents were not that house so much maybe I can be
me be
It's happening It's happening now now now Quick Quick keys keys
can never find keys where are the KEYS
Hi hihihi
Hi-

hello

there's a thread running from me
to you

Is this what I imagined life was Yes I suppose
walks
Lots of walks Long walks
Prams Pushchairs Cakes with Candles
Are these my images or ones we're all given
  You can't control what she does or where she goes you of all people
                                                       should know
                         It's the way she talks to me
                                     Well
                      I never spoke to you like that
                                        Well!

                    Look after yourself
                    You know you can't
                    I won't be fussed over
                    Well the doctors-
                    I'm sick of doctors
     Well I should think you are but that doesn't change
             The finish on the casket if you'd like a different hue
No that's fine this is all fine and the flowers- He wasn't fussed about
flowers Why would anyone want to be buried not (burnt) cremated I
told him he was mad but that's what he wanted and everyone else
           Everyone always looking at me out the
           corner of their eye as if I've never
           I'm fine

                                            Fine
           Everything's fine everything's always fine
            everyone dies and it's fine and it's fine and
            the house will be quieter but I'll always have
And what do you think you saw
I told you
But you didn't-
I said I came home and my brother was sitting on the sofa There

Your brother-
David Was his name
I remember- But-
Stop talking to me like that
Like what
Like I'm a Lonely Old Woman seeing things
It's just-
I know how it sounds but I'm telling you I'm not interested in whether ghosts exist or where whatever goes or what it means or anything what to do with it I'm not going to bring people here with machines to scan the place for ectojism
Plasm mum
I'm just telling you what I saw which was my brother sitting on the sofa Looking at me
Did he talk to you
No and what would he say nothing to say nothing to say likely look after your brother I tried I tried to look after you I think of you all the time I can't get through a day without thinking of you I think of you I think
I think you're the most important person in my life and you're dead and I never spoke to you much when you were alive and I would understand it if you felt the need to haunt me if that's what that was what this is haunt me all you like I don't mind it'd be nice to have someone to watch the tv with of an evening time

> *Isn't really on your side here (everyonedies) and any operations we could do would only buy you a little more time and it'd be time you wouldn't enjoy much either*
> *Well you can't just*
> *I'll do as I like it's my life-*
> *But they*
> *They*
> *told me what They told me and that's that there's no use getting in a tizz about it-*
> *Mum*

> *Mummummummummummummothermothermothermother mothergrandmothergrandgrandmamumumumumumumu mumumumumumumumumnnnnnn*
> *not going to one of those places no matter what you say*

but it's the only place they can
I know I'm a burden
You're not a burden
A burden I'm a burden (everyone dies) a burden that can't won't
See it's not so bad the window looks out onto the lawns there
Yes lovely thank you
never liked gardening gardens flowers don't understand the appeal
an utterly shallow exercise as far as I can see what do you do once
you've made a garden just sit and stare at it and realise your head's
as empty as it was before
Ah!
AH!
No don't bring her let her see me in here too much let her think of me
in better shape I really
don't mind David's here with me
Well let her think that if it helps what am I supposed to
Mum I love you
Mum I love you
I love you, Mum
I love you I love you I love you I love you
I love you I love you I love you
I'm so embarrassed I wish I could tell them to leave and not watch
the next bit whatever the next bit is dark
It's dark

It's dark

IT'S DARK wetwetnesswetwetmyselfhorribledon't looknoNONO
quiet always quiet here so
quiet
see the corners melting can you
think i had a good life but its hard to tell really i don't have anything
to compare
might have been happier at times but then probably everyone could
have
regrets i have regrets (look after your brother) it's fine to have regrets
i'm allowed No Regrets is what people say but that's a fridge magnet
i think
oh OH there are no edges to anything

driving to work can't see the sides of the road all slipping away from me i have a new coat stop kissing me and there's wallpaper on the ceiling
on the ceiling it's so strange there's red
Red Rushing Close Closer And I can smell mum's
Jumper
Can't
hands and hands my hands press pressing
this is all very
red red rushing In Red
Rushing
Rushing
Rushing
Rushing
-

With thanks to The MacDowell Colony, where this was written.

Northleigh, 1940

Northleigh, 1940 was first performed at the Royal Court Jerwood Theatre Downstairs, Sloane Square, on Tuesday, 6 June 2023, with the following cast and creative team:

Kate O'Flynn

Director Sam Pritchard
Designer Merle Hensel
Lighting Designer Elliot Griggs
Sound Artist & Composer Melanie Wilson
Video Designer Lewis den Hertog

*to be read aloud,
by one performer.*

German section translated by John Birke

I was there:

> *Alone, on ashen sands that yearned beyond*
> *All measure known in realms familiar.*
> *Where rolling waves of black immensity*
> *Were born from flames of death's obsidian hue,*
> *And rising plumes became a furious sky*
> *That glowered down upon my naked form.*
>
> *And from this shore of sights impossible*
> *I stood, and saw gigantic beasts tear through*
> *The canopy and fall: The writhing shapes*
> *Of whails uncountable, made up of souls*
> *Innumerable, with limbs and torsos wricked*
> *Into these plunging, tarred leviathans.*
>
> *These beasts were legion as unearthly rain*
> *And as each one collided with the sea*
> *Their forms were all dispersed- now shapeless crowds*
> *That swirled and wept in pained cacophony*
> *And lurched towards the shore in tides of grief*
> *Until their pallid flesh did crawl on land.*
>
> *I turned and made my way across dark plains*
> *Where figures stood aghast as monuments,*
> *Caught petrified through misery and awe.*
> *Their kind did rouse my curiosity-*
> *But one I held to speak with I found mute-*
> *A withered leg fused wetly to his throat.*
>
> *And as I walked their numbers built until*
> *There came to be deep woods of men entire,*
> *Within which soon their flesh did fall away*
> *Until the trunks were tow'ring spinal chords*
> *Lubricious, quiv'ring up towards the sky*
> *Each planted in grim hollows of putrescence.*
>
> *I feared that I was swallowed in this place-*
> *But then emerged to stand beneath a wall-*
> *A face of rock unblinking, worn with time,*

The surface rife with holes my grip might hold.
And high above I thought I spied some hope-
Some precious light that tempted my escape.

And so I dared to climb and leave behind
That cursed earth where nothing good held root.
Whilst far above the sky began to roil,
Soon hurling down cruel floods that froze my skin;
The stone becoming slick, my grip in doubt-
I clung with desperation to the wall

As through this endless deluge it became
A coursing waterfall which charged to cause
My tumbling back below. And as I held
I felt each socket fill with tumorous growth,
As bulbous eyes that swelled within each hole

Did leer at me as though perhaps had enough to buy her own gramophone so she wouldn't have to use the one downstairs. They couldn't be too dear- she could look for one in the newspaper. She only listened to records when the house was empty but with her own player she could play them at night, under the blankets.

It was late. How late she didn't know as her alarm clock was turned to the wall. If she knew what time it was she'd feel obliged to sleep. This habit of clinging to the night cost her each day. Falling asleep at her typewriter. Her pay docked. The other girls smirking to each other. Rolling their eyes. It had gotten worse since getting the earlier bus.

She pushed aside the strewn paperbacks and crawled down the bed to the window, lifting the heavy curtain away from the glass. The street was silent. As if a painting. She squinted through the gloom at the houses lined up opposite, each identical to the one she was crouched within. A shape darted across the road. Out hunting. Wake to a corpse in the kitchen no doubt.

She let the curtain fall back to rest and began with reluctance to clear the bed. Photographs of severe men stared out from back covers. They were writers. They were born and lived in places with interesting names. American names. Providence. Auburn. They wrote about worlds imagined, worlds of fear and death. Pressed them onto cheap paper so she might gather them onto shelves; constellations of ink.

Her lunchbreak each day was spent at the same bookstall on Church Street. It was far enough away to take almost the entire break getting there and back, and so she ate her sandwiches whilst she walked, eyes fixed on her shoes, advancing along her route with mindless precision. Upon arrival the creased spines were interrogated with prejudice, each book needing to make a strong case for her purchase. Most days the seller pointed her to the women's section as if she were lost. She didn't know if this was a point he was making or if he'd just never committed her to memory.

The day's book smuggled back in her purse, the afternoon then spent fearing its discovery. One of the girls bringing it in from the cloakroom to show the others- the crude illustrations of tentacled monsters on the cover somehow confirming everything they'd assumed about her.

She sat at the desk in the pool's exact centre. Elaine and Ruth occupied the positions to her left and right, and spoke through her all day as if she were porous. Elaine's husband was in Egypt. Each letter sent home was read aloud in abridged form to the entire office, the passages concerning his physical intentions for her redacted but alluded to with blushing laughter. Elaine had cruel eyes but beautiful wrists. She held each letter up with gloved fingers, laughter vibrating through her, a tiny mole dashing in and out of view from within her sleeve.

It was too late to run a bath.
She hadn't heard him go to bed. Perhaps she'd fallen asleep reading.

Now her mother was gone she could stay in the water as long as she liked. Lie there for hours, skin pruning, staring down at the parts of herself breaking the surface. Previously her reveries would be broken by her mother's voice through the door, or, once bedbound, shouted from the next room.

Her father never disturbed her. Whilst dressing one night she spied him from the window, limping to the hedge at the end of the garden.

She had spent so long reading about death it was a shock to find how mundane it was in reality. There was no poetry to it. It was corridors and soiled sheets and bowls of thick phlegm marbled with blood. There was no newfound humility or perspective, and her mother's last days were as full of exhortations to speak up as all those that had gone before. Finally she had collapsed into herself, a full body frown. Bodies were built from meat and optimism.

She knew he wanted to talk more now they were alone, but nothing had loosened. The silence between them was terrible and leaden, so much so that waiting at the bus stop together each day became unbearable, and so she told him her shift had changed. She now caught the first bus into town alone, and walked the streets for the two hours before the office opened, slipping inside when the cleaners arrived. It was one of these mornings she found the orphaned glove in the cloakroom.

She dangled down to look under the bed.
Her mother had berated her endlessly for the state of her 'cave' as she called it, yet wouldn't trust her to clean it herself. Beneath the bed was now thick with dust and cat hair, signifiers of her absence. The glove lived under the carpet she'd pried loose in the far corner. Some nights she was sure she could feel it, throbbing up through the mattress.
She didn't think her mother had ever had an internal life.

A scratch at the door brought her to her feet. Wide eyes stared up at her from ankle-height. No mouse tonight. The cat slunk past and leapt onto the bed, pawing at the blankets. Out on the landing she saw light leaking up from below.
She crept downstairs, realizing with surprise that the dining room was the source. Pushing the door open she thought it empty at first, before spying shoes visible through the mesh of the Morrison Shelter. One smaller than the other.

— Dad?

— You made me jump.
— What are you doing?
— Nothing.
  Just checking it still fits.

— Are you alright?
— Fine, fine.

— I was just heading up to bed, and I glanced in here, at it, and
  I thought I'd crawl in for a minute.
  I didn't expect to be caught.

— You can come in, if you like.
— Why?
— Well- Just-

— Try it out yourself.

— There.
  Would've had a job squeezing three of us in, eh?

— I'd have had an Anderson.
  Your mother didn't want the garden digging up.
  Not sure why having this great thing sat in the house is any better.

— *You could get one now.*
— *No, no.*
  This is fine.
  They say it can stand your whole house dropping on it.
  That's what does for you, course. Not the bombs.

— *Do you know what the time is?*
— *No.*

— *Maggie came and looked in at me.*
  Must have thought I'd left my senses.
  Like you.
— *I didn't think that.*

— *Were you up reading?*
— *Yes.*
— *What's it this time?*
— *Just stories.*
— *Ghouls and goblins.*
— *Something like that.*

— *That's what'd finish you off. Buried under all your books.*
  It'd be like Smith's falling on you.
— *It's not that many.*

— *We could put a picture up- On the roof of it, here.*
  So you're not just staring at nothing.

*A watercolour or something, you know. Landscape.
Give you something to take your mind off things, should
Jerry come.*

— *Course we could just read. Bring the paper in.*

— *Hey- We'll be needing a cake next week.*
— *I don't need one.*
— *It's no trouble. I'll order one in at the baker's.*
— *A whole cake's too much for two people.*
— *I'm sure I'll manage to polish it off.*

— *I like a cake.*

— *Thirty, eh?
Blimey.*

— *Thirty.*

— *How are you finding your early starts?*
— *They're fine.*
— *Got you working late now, too.*
— *Only sometimes.*
— *Ships in the night, aren't we.*

— *Thirty years old...*

— *Thirty-*
— *I'll move out soon.*

— What's that?

— I won't be here much longer. I'll move out.
— Oh-
— I'll get married.
— Married?

— Is that what you want?

— That's how it's meant to be.

— I don't mind you being here.

— I don't mind you getting married, either. If that's what you want.

— Just-
Whatever you like.

— Are you unhappy, do you think?
— No-
— Alright-
— I'm fine-
— You're quiet, is all.
—That's just how I am.
There's nothing wrong with me.

— I didn't say there was anything wrong with you.

— I wouldn't ever say that.

*— I don't think you should worry what you're meant to do.
You do as you like.*

*— I think people spend far too much time thinking like that.
Meant by who? I don't see why that's how things should be.
Spending all your time doing things you don't like.
I never wanted to be a clerk for a cotton company.
That's not anything that ever crossed my mind. And now look-
Spend more time doing that than anything else.
Don't think I'm even much good at it.*

— What would you do if you didn't.

— Didn't what.
— If you didn't have to do your job.

— I'd listen to my records.
— You can't get paid to do that.
*— No, but-
If I didn't need to be paid.
I'd just listen to my records.
All day, probably.*

*— Your mother'd go spare.
She used to give me a right earful for spending my wages on records.
Quite right, of course.*

— What would you do. If you weren't a typist.

— I don't know.
— You could write your own stories.
— No...
— You could do that now, yourself. That's how they'll all start- Writing at night after their other jobs. I'll bet you'd be good at it.
— I tried.
— There you are.
— I wasn't good.
All the voices just sounded like me.

— That doesn't sound so bad.

— She wasn't nice to you.

— Who wasn't?

— Your mother? When?
— All the time.
— No...
— Picking at you- Shouting at you-
— No, that wasn't-
— You just said- She was always getting at you-
— That's just- Mithering. Bossing about.
— In the hospital still-
— She was in pain-
— She didn't like us.
— That's not true.
— She didn't like me.
— That's not true.

— You shouldn't think that.

— She could be a little hard on us, maybe.

— But like we're saying-
  Things don't turn out the way you thought.
  I'm sure she didn't dream of marrying a cripple when she was a young girl.
— Don't say that about yourself.
— Why not? If the shoe fits. Haha.

— People still look at me like I made my leg this way.
  So I wouldn't have to sign up.
  I'd go if they'd have me.
— You're too old.
— I'm not so old-
— Too old to join up.
— I tried to go the first time but they turned me away.
  Put a feather through my mum's door. That's what they thought of me.

— Funny how they think something's wrong with your body there must be something wrong with your head, too.

— Course, maybe they're right.

— Stopped me talking to people growing up. Boys my age.
  Used to be with the girls more.
  Though I was more their pet than anything else.
  Then when the boys and girls started looking at each other neither of them wanted me around. Looking at me like they could catch it.

— Your mother never looked at me any way I didn't like.
  She'd get cross with me in the summer-
  When I wouldn't roll up my trouser legs on the beach.

Didn't like me hiding myself.

— *I don't remember that.*

—*She'd wait till you were off swimming.*
  Didn't want you thinking your dad didn't like himself.

— *I miss her.*

— *They told me not to go early tomorrow.*

— *Oh right?*

— *Back on the number five then.*
— *Yes.*
— *Righto.*

— *Here, what do you say to a quick sandwich before turning in?*
  I've a space I could fill-

                              (An air raid siren is heard)

— *Crikey-*

— *We're in the right place, at least.*
  Funny timing, eh?
  Here, my heart's going-
— *It's alright.*
— *I know, but, you can't help-*
— *You said it can stand the whole house-*

— Well that's what they tell you.
— So they must know. They'll do tests.

— Dad.
— I've got to get Maggie- Your mother'd never forgive me-
— No, wait-
— I'll just be-
— She's here- Look-
— Mkgnao!
— Daft puss- In you come - You knew to come, eh-
— Breathe Dad.
— I'm breathing- I know how to breathe-
— It's alright.
— Yes.
— We're safe.
— Yes.
— Here, hold my-

form plötzlich fremdartig gehalten in sternlosigkeit hunderte tauchen auf ragen auf das ungebärdige raster dort unten scheu verhüllt, beide flächen verweigertes spiegelbild der andern, künden alle von der welle der boten die ihre jungen herbeitragen durch die nacht übers wasser jetzt

drop
down
downward
wailing
hurtling
spin-sinking
riders of velocity
flesh prior come panels
rivets
remade with women's fingers find
fins fixed now in furious descent
death dealing
she's his is how she can type
couldn't for toffee told her talk herself higher
hassling heckling hounding holed up hiding
didn't i dread heading home and she the same now

gravity galloping grim-faced parasite pieces inside yourself
despite your efforts even
held your hair alike the end neverthe never
had a father the kind she does did
decent man mine a mute drunk didn't notice him half the time
till he
took against him course
curled lips cross the floor case you hadn't
never saw the not wanting an athlete
expected somehow always
plain jane to your sister still
last laugh limping down the aisle
barren whilst you bore fruit
and always handsome no one noticed
had a hunger so
good when he put his mind to
trailed fingers up thighs
took hold him in picture houses below
blushes but just about drove the headboard through the wall
warmth weaving
falling
turning
terminal
told him not to talk himself the way he would
then she the same
back bent in apology
brought bile to your tongue
stand straight
sit smart
try untie knots made in utero no
not his fault you can't let be
shake her so she sees what you do
how you lay awake alone abed so young
made promises to plaster that she'd
never want the way you did and
swore to sing the songs your house had not
to show her how she mattered most

and spit the pips they'd planted so as not to pass your
poisoned parts
but through they flow regardless rivers running
ice and acid all they gave to give away
and everything you couldn't say
to let her know
to stop her sending chin to chest
how much
how all
new colours never known before her
ships had landed on your shore
through his becoming
pulling
pressing into me
sweet hum of our machinery
come calling her to climb
through waters rushing witness
crowded coursing t'wards the
reaching spires the
cobwebbed cobbled streets the
brick bay-windowed homes here huddled
'gainst this falling ocean come as
easy as the rain she
spills out slick between your thighs
she crawls to feed
she meets your eyes
the roof tiles' choral rattle sung
the overture done
here they come-

Zero for the Young Dudes!

Zero for the Young Dudes! was first performed as part of National Theatre Connections 2017

Notes on the text

To be staged with a cast of any number of performers.

Genders in each scene have been assigned randomly and should be changed to fit the cast.

Most scenes have a specific number of characters speaking but this can be altered by assigning the lines differently.

The entire cast should appear in Scenes One, Two and Sixteen.

The same actor should perform Scenes Six, Eleven and Fifteen.

The setting is a summer camp.

The time is now.

Maybe the performers wear a uniform or matching outfits. Maybe the performers remain on stage throughout.

Maybe blackouts would be respite and should be avoided unless stated.

Maybe the audience are the enemy.

A question without a question mark denotes a flatness of tone.

- Indicates an interruption of speech or train of thought.

... Indicates either a trailing off, a breather, a shift, or a transition.

/ Indicates where the next line of dialogue interrupts or overlaps.

{ } Contains dialogue not heard by the audience.

One.
RISE.

The **Campers** *eat cereal.*

They occasionally eye the audience.

Whisper/mutter.

Laugh at something secret.

It's somewhat threatening but hard to tell why.

When the bell or buzzer yells they stand and head to leave
a rabble
half
draining bowls of milk
half
hollering laughing pushing.

Two.
PLEDGE.

The **Campers** *line up to pledge in unison:*

> I PLEDGE MY TRUE ALLEGIANCE
> TO THE NATION THAT SHELTERS, CLOTHES,
> AND FEEDS ME.
>
> LAND OF MY BIRTH,
> HOME OF MY PEOPLE,
> WHOSE VALUES AND BELIEFS I SHARE,
> AND WHOSE LAWS I UPHOLD AND OBEY.
>
> I AM GRATEFUL TO BE A CITIZEN OF A COUNTRY
> SO PROSPEROUS, FAIR, AND FREE;
> AND SHALL GIVE UNCONDITIONAL OBEDIENCE
> AND RESPECT
> TO THOSE THAT SEEK TO SECURE

A BRIGHT AND RIGHTEOUS FUTURE

FOR ME

AND ALL THAT FOLLOW.

I PLEDGE MY LIFE AND BLOOD TO THIS CAUSE,

SO HELP ME GOD.

Three.

RUN.

A clearing in the woods that look over the camp.
Two **Campers** *are here in shorts and t-shirts.*
One holds a hand grenade proudly, showing the other.

— When though?
— This morning.
— Just this morning?
— I said.
— Under your pillow?
— Under my pillow, I said.

Pause.

— Four others, too-
— Four others have them?
— At least.
— You saw?
— No-
— You actually didn't *see* though.
— No, but I know because there's, there's like a *nod*-
— You're nodding at each other.
— We're not *nodding* at each other, we're just, you see someone, across the dinner hall or whatever, and you see them, and you look at them, and you just. . . (*Nod.*)
— And that means-
— That means you both, you both *know*.
— That you both have them.
— That we both have them.

Pause.

— Are we allowed them?
— No, we're not allowed them, we're not allowed shoelaces, why would we be allowed grenades?
— But how come you have one then?
— Because I found it under my-
— Yeah, but how *come* though?
— Because someone's putting them under pillows in the dorms-
— Yeah, but *why*?

Pause.

— Is there a plan?
— . . .
— Is there a plan no one told us about?

. . .

Like a secret plan. For the whole camp.

. . .

Do you think?
— I dunno.

Pause.

— Does it smell?
— (*Sniffs.*) No. Not much, anyway.
— Is it new?
— Looks it.
— Looks pretty new.
It's from our war, you think? Not some old war.
— Maybe. . .

Beat.

— Can I hold it?
— Get your own.
— I don't have my own though!
— Put a note under your pillow.
— I just wanna hold it for a few seconds.

. . .

Just for like five seconds.

. . .

Please.

. . .

Just for one second.

Pause.

The grenade is handed over.

— Wow.

She walks around, holding it aloft, rapt.
Inspects it.

— That bit pings off.
— Duh.
— You pull the pin and then when you let it go, that bit pings off.
— I know already.
— We never had these before. . .

Pause.

— OK, give it back now.
— (*Miming throwing it.*) Bloody Japs!
— You had it long enough-
— Bloody Japs! Kamikazes!

It's snatched back.

— Knob.
— (*Grins.*)
— Japs?
— It's racist for Japanese.
— I know.
— When d'ya think they'll tell you the plan?
— I don't know there *is* a plan.
— I bet there is. You don't hand out grenades without a plan.

. . .

Maybe we're going to war again.

— . . .

336 Zero for the Young Dudes!

I dunno.

. . .

Someone's coming.

Another **Camper** *runs on.*

— What are you dildos doing- What's that?
— Nothing-
— It's a hand grenade.
— Oh. (*Beat.*) Have you got a fag?
— No.
— Pfft.

She shoves her hands down her shorts and rustles around.

— I hate cross-country.

Produces a cigarette and lighter after much rummaging, lights it.

— You'll get done if they catch you smoking.
— My socks are wet as fuck. . .

Four.

WASH.

The **Campers** *stand with towels, queuing for the showers.*
Two **Campers** *talk as the line occasionally moves forward a few steps.*

— The jeeps?
— The jeeps they patrol-
— Yeah, I know which jeeps you mean, but how are you gonna get one of them?
— Because sometimes they just, when they need to run into the office quickly they leave them running outside sometimes-
— Not often though.
— Sometimes they do.
— Not often though.
— Well say they do, they do one day-

— For like thirty seconds.
— So in those thirty seconds I get in it and I drive-
— You can't drive.
— I can drive.
— You don't have a licence-
— You don't *need* a licence to drive.
— Yes you do.
— Well, legally, yeah, you have to be twenty-one and have a licence, but what I'm saying is that anyone *can* drive, it's not a hard thing to do.
— I dunno...
— It's easy!
— There's the clutch, and...
— Trust me, I can drive. I drive the jeep. I wait till they leave it outside the office and I get in and drive it-
— And you just happen to be there when that happens.
— I take my moment- I take my moment and I drive, I drive away wicked fast-
— They're shooting at you-
— And I'm weaving the car-
— You're dodging bullets.
— I'm not *dodging* bullets, I'm just weaving the car, I'm *weaving* it.
— You're getting shot all over-
— I'm not-
— You're like (*Rattling with the impact of a hundred rifles.*) uhuhuhuhuhuhuh-
— I might get *some* minor injuries.
— Your guts all fall out-
— My guts don't fall out-

Another **Camper** *has come on, looking lost.*

— Is this where we go to get our orders?
— Join the queue.
— How come we have to get them in the showers?
— / It's-

— We're having a conversation here.
— But I don't have my towel, I can't-

Others in the line start piping up:

— Hey, no pushing in-
— Who's pushing in?
— Get to the back of the line.
— Move it, dude.

He heads to the back of the line.

— So you're driving-
— Did everyone else get a grenade?
— / Shhh-
— Shut the fuck up, what's wrong with you?
— Moron.

Beat.

— Where do you drive.
— I drive up the hill, up to the woods, where we do cross-country.
— Your guts are hanging out. . .
— My guts are not hanging out.
— You've lost an eye-
— I've got both eyes.
— You're mowing down kids doing cross-country-
— I'm *driving* up there, where the most isolated section of fence is.
— And what?
— And I smash straight through it with the jeep.

Beat.

— What.
— I smash into it-
— It's not one fence, it's three.
— I smash through *them*-
— And razor-wire, and those things with the spikes-
— I'll be going a hundred miles an hour.

— And it's electric.

— ...

Then-

— That kid ran into it last week and burst all over the place.

— Well, then, I'll-

...

Okay,

So,

I'll take the big-

You know the big tarp sheet things we cover the track with when it rains?

— Yeah.

— I'll have one of those in the jeep-

— So you have to roll up this huge sheet thing.

— I do that before.

— And carry it, have it with you-

— Yeah-

— At the exact moment the jeep is free for thirty seconds-

— I-

— And in those thirty seconds you have to get this thing, I mean, they're *huge*, those sheets, they cover the whole track-

— I throw it in the jeep, I drive up to the woods, I stop at the fence, I throw the tarp over the fence so I don't *touch* it, then I climb up and over and out!

Pause.

— Then what.

— Then,

eventually,

I go round and free all the other camps-

— All of them.

— One at a time.

— Just on your own?

— I've got fantastic muscles and fabulous reflexes.

— There's a few holes in this plan.

— I free the Titches first, because they have the least security. I get them out and then I have a small army to help me free the

others, free our Generals and everything, and then once everyone else is free, I come back here, I *lead* everyone back here (cos by this point they've all voted and made me a General), and we come and we storm *this* camp, and the counsellors and the guards are all like 'Hey, isn't that the kid who escaped just-' BLEGH- Head shot!
— This is not even a plan.
— It's a brilliant plan.

Another **Camper** *has come on:*

— Is this where / we-
— (*Both.*) *Yes.*
— It's a terrible plan.
— It's better than whatever it is they've got planned tonight.
— You don't even know what we're doing yet.
— It won't be as good as mine.
— The point is to make a big gesture, not just have one of us escape. There's no point doing anything if they don't even notice.
— They'd notice-
— London wouldn't. Kids escape all the time- Or they're shot *trying* to escape.
They don't report it in the capital.
— How do you know?
— Because why would they?
— I reckon I could cause enough of a stir-
— No way.

Another **Camper** *has come on:*

— Is this where we get our orders?
— Why is everyone asking me?
— You're tall.
— How come we have to get them in the showers?
— Do we have to get naked?
— I have a verruca-

— Can everyone shut up? They're just over there, you wanna give everything away?
— The showers are the only place they don't watch us.
— They're scared of people thinking they're paedos so they don't go in the showers, okay?
— Someone did a big shit on the floor in there last week and no one cleaned it up and all the water made it spread round everywhere.
— Yeah, well,
that's the downside.

Five.

DIRT.

There is a huge pile of earth.
*Two **Campers** are steadily moving it from one side of the stage to the other.*
They shovel up a pile, walk it across the stage, and dump it on the growing new pile.

— Sometimes I even forget how long I've been here!
Sometimes I try and, like I'll think, hey, how long *has* it been? And I can't even remember!
I remember how many times I've moved this pile from here to there, but I didn't have to do it every day, and they only started making me do it about a year ago so I can't work it out from that. How long have you been here?
— Three months, seventeen days.
— You see, you're smart cos I bet you started counting when you got here, but I didn't even think to *do* that. It was so long ago, and I never actually moved camp, I've always been in this one, this is the only camp I was ever even *in*. My unit got cornered in this supermarket and they rounded us up and brought us here and most of them got moved to other places but I'm still here, I've been

here the whole time so it's just a big blur with how much time it actually is, and obviously they don't let you have calendars here, or watches, and there's only the clocks in the dorms and the dinner hall so you can't even really keep track that easy. Some of the kids in my dorm keep scratch-marks on their beds so they know, you know? But I never did that.

They move dirt in silence for a while.

— Sometimes I even forget where I came from in the first place! Haha!

They move dirt in silence for a while.

— Sometimes when I try and remember what it was like before I have a total brainfart. All I can remember is the guns, because I used to work with the armoury? So I'll be trying to remember what toys I used to have when I was really small, but my head'll just be all like M4 Carbine, M4A1, AK47, SA80, L7A2 GPMG, L115A3, M80,
And I don't think I had any of those when I was little, unless maybe I had very liberal parents! Haha!

She laughs for a while.

— Oh. . .boy.

They move dirt in silence for a while.

— My parents died in the bombings.

They move dirt in silence for a while.

— Sometimes it even gets in my head when I'm not *trying* to remember.
Like they'll be asking me a question in class, or I'll be in the queue for lunch or doing the pledge or something, and my head'll just be like M4 Carbine, M4 Carbine, M4CarbineM4CarbineM4Carbine, over and over and over making me go mental, or I'll just be totally obsessively thinking of this guy's head I saw blown up once,
or this finger I found on the floor of a bank we stormed and my brain'll just be like fingerfingerfingerfingerfingerfingerfingerfinger, you know?

And then whoever asked the question or whatever, they'll be trying to get my attention, but I'll just be totally spaced out, and not saying anything, and I'll mess up, and I think that's why I get dirt duty a lot.

...

I never actually obsess on the things that happen *in* the camp, just the things in the war, isn't that weird?

...
...

Do you like Harry Potter?

— (*Shrugs.*) It's alright.

— Dumbledore's the coolest!

I once had a dream where I was a wizard, 'cept it wasn't like Harry Potter, I wasn't at Hogwarts or anything, I was just here in the camp 'cept I had magic powers, and I was using them to zap all the guards and the counsellors and then I used my wand to bust the fences, some of the fences I could melt with a special spell I had, oh and also I was flying? And then we all got freed and all of us were running out of the camp all cheering and everyone was shouting my name because I was the hero, but then when we got outside everyone's head just suddenly started melting! Everyone stopped running and there was this kind of *fizzing* sound and then everyone's head was all just bubbling and popping like Rice Crispies and their eyes were drooping down their heads and their mouths went from big smiles to big frowns and everyone was like, grabbing at their heads saying No! No! Don't melt my head! And they all thought it was *me*, because *I* was the one with the magic! They were all looking up at me with their runny eyes saying Don't! Stop! Stop melting our heads! Why would you free us just to melt our heads?! And I'm like I didn't, I didn't! I'm trying to tell them it's not me, it's not my fault, but their ears have all melted so they can't even *hear* me ! So I try to do a spell that'll make their heads go back to normal except now it's like all my magic is *gone*, I can't do magic any more for some reason, but it's too late anyway because now everyone's head is just a big pink puddle on their necks and they're all falling down dead. And then the last one who

still has half a head comes up to me and he was trying to keep the shape of it like he was trying to hold melting ice cream into some kind of structure and he looks at me with his eyes that are like dripping yolks and his mouth was all waxy like a candle and he just looks straight at me and just says-
Why?

. . .

And then he falls down dead like the rest.

. . .

. . .

. . .

What do you think that means?

— . . .

(*Shrugs.*)

I dunno.

They move dirt in silence for a while.

— How long did they give you?
— Four hours.
— Me too! What for?
— I did a shit in the shower.
— Wow! That takes confidence!

Well I bet this four hours is gonna pass by like nobody's business. They think it's some big punishment to make us do this until our legs don't work any more but I actually take a lot of pleasure from it. Once I get all the dirt from this side to that side I always take a moment and look at it, even if they yell at me, because I like to take a second and notice the impact I can have on the world and the elements around me. Don't you think?

It's much better than solitary too, in solitary it's just so *boring*. No one to talk to. Just *quiet*. *Quiet* all the time.

Quietquietquiet. I mean, sure, that's great if you just want some peace, and actually I do sometimes want peace and quiet, but not when I'm on dirt duty, no way, I like to really cut loose out here. And we have so much in common we can just talk the time away.

Zero for the Young Dudes! 345

We can talk about all kinds of interesting subjects!
Like we can talk about *food*, and what *friends* we have, and what types of clothes we used to wear, and we can tell our war stories, and we can talk about *cats*, and we can talk about keeping fit, and we can talk about the other camps you were at and do like *comparisons* and we can talk about ghosts and scary stories, and we can talk about politics and we can talk about *fruit* and we can talk about where we used to live and we can talk about people we know that *died* and we can talk about *space,* and we can talk about *hair products-*
— Why'd you get dirt duty.
— Talking too much. Hey, what's your favourite type of smell?

Six.

▮▮▮▮▮▮.

Dear Mum,

I am having a really ▮▮▮▮▮▮ time at camp. The counsellors are all ▮▮▮▮▮▮ and one of them told me ▮▮▮▮▮▮▮▮▮▮.

I'm sure learning a lot about ▮▮▮▮▮▮ and ▮▮▮▮▮▮. There is a lot of time to ▮▮▮▮▮▮▮▮ in here.

I have ▮▮▮▮▮▮▮▮, and in ▮▮▮▮▮▮ we get to ▮▮▮▮▮▮ in the lake and ▮▮▮▮▮▮▮▮ and sometimes we ▮▮▮▮▮▮▮▮▮▮.

Don't ▮▮▮▮▮▮▮▮.

If they decide ▮▮▮▮▮▮▮▮▮▮▮▮, then know that I ▮▮▮▮▮▮▮▮▮▮. And that everything ▮▮▮▮▮▮▮▮ has ▮▮▮▮▮▮ into ▮▮▮▮▮▮ and I am ready ▮▮▮▮▮▮▮▮▮▮.

All my ▮▮▮▮▮▮,
▮▮▮▮▮▮.

Seven.

SOLITARY.

In solitary confinement, a **Camper** *bounces a ball off the walls.*

We watch this for a while.

— Hey.

Pause.

— Hey.
— (*Unseen, outside.*) What.
— How long am I in here for again?

Pause.

— How long am I-
— Two days.
— Two *days*?

. . .

Actual full days?

Pause.

— How long have I done so far?

Pause.

— I said how long-
— Twenty minutes.
— Twenty *minutes*?

. . .

That can't- Twenty minutes, really?

He tries to count the remainder but struggles.

Pause.

He goes back to bouncing the ball.

— How long till lunch?

Pause.

— I said how lo / ng-
— A long time.
— Yeah, but *how* long?

Pause.

— How long though?
. . .
How long though?
. . .
How long till lunch though?
. . .
How long till-
— I'm not allowed to talk to you.
— How come?

Pause.

— How come you're not?
— Because you're in solitary.
— Yeah, but. . .
. . .

Pause.

He bounces the ball for a while.

— How long has it been now?
— I'm not telling you every- What's that noise in there?
— What?
— What are you making noise with?
— This?

He bounces the ball.

— What is that.
— It's a ball.

Beat.

— A ball?
— Yeah.
— You have a ball in there?

— Yeah.
— You're not supposed to have a ball in there.
— Why not?
— Because you're not.
— Why though?
— Because it's solitary.
— Yeah, but, I gotta have *some*thing to do.
— You're not allowed to have a ball in there-
— How old are you?

Beat.

— How old / are-
— I'm not allowed to talk to you.
— Why?
. . .
Are you a grown-up?
— Yes.
— You don't sound like it.
— I am-
— How old are you then?

Pause.

— Like thirty. . .?
— I'm twenty-one.
— Pfft. That's not that old.
— Stop talking.
— That's not that old at all.

Pause.

— Were you on their side or our side?
. . .
Whose side were you on?
Before.
. . .
Nineteen, twenty, twenty-one. . . You must have been on our side, right? If you're only twenty-one now.

...
You were with us, yeah?

Pause.

— Did you have to go through this camp?

...
Did you do one of the camps before you worked here?
— What's it to you.
— I'm interested.

Pause.

— Yes.
— You did?
— Yes.

Pause.

— Did it work?
Like it's s'posed to?

...
Did it, like, change you to being on their side?
— There's no sides.
— Yeah, right.

...
Were you captured or did you turn yourself in?

Pause.

— You still there. . .?
— I'm not talking to you any more.

Pause.

He bounces the ball again.

— I bet you did really well to get to be a guard.

...
You must've only just got out, too. They only let you out when you're twenty-one. And only then if you did well.

...
Were you one of those ones that did their whole dorm in?

King Rat?

. . .

Do you wanna be a counsellor one day?

. . .

Do you wanna be like the ones / who-
— What are you in here for.
— What?
— Why are you in solitary.

Beat.

— . . .

I wouldn't pull this kid's fingernails out.
— Why not.
— . . .

(*Shrugs.*) I dunno.

. . .

Didn't want to.

. . .

Maybe that's how come I won't get to be a guard like you.
I bet you did anything they-
— Shut up.
— Hey, are you worried what'll happen to you if there's a breakout?

. . .

Some kids hate the ones who turned even more than the actual grown-ups.

. . .

Are you worried we'll do all the things to you that your lot are making us do to each other?
I bet it'll-
— Be *quiet*.

Pause.

He bounces the ball some more.

Looks around.

He shoves his hands down his pants and pulls his grenade out. Inspects it.
Picks his nose.

— What time is it now?

Eight.
FEED.

In the dinner hall.
Two **Campers** *serve the lunch line. The one in charge wears an eye patch.*

The lunchline passes in front of them, a few **Campers** *at a time.*

— He's a traitor.
— For *that*?
— If he doesn't do it then *they* do it.
— Yeah, but-
— You've not got one? She hasn't got one-

The **Second Camper** *hands a grenade to a* **Camper** *in line.*

— Vi / va la revolucion.
— Viva la revolucion.
— We all agreed.
— Yeah-
— We *all* agreed. No more violence at their hands.
— I get all that-
— If I'm having my fingernails dragged out, I want it done by one of my brothers or sisters, looking into their eyes and knowing it's an unwilling act, done with compassion and solidarity. I don't want my body mutilated by my oppressors. My enemy.
— He was a Titch-
— So?
— So you can do that to a six-year-old?
— I can do it knowing the alternative is worse.
He *still* got his nails pulled out, except now by one of *them*.

And they *enjoy* it.

. . .

It's all the same anyway.

. . .

They put some of us in one type of school, the others another. Some of us get healthcare, some of us don't.
They always wanted us at war with ourselves, consuming ourselves, all they've done here is made the process more honest. And I'll take a brutal honesty over a lie.

— You're unbelievable.

— You're an idealist.

— *I'm* an idealist? You thought we could set up the new state without an economy-

— Because we would have.

— An economy is a, a, it happens *naturally*,

— Him, him-

The **Second Camper** *hands out a grenade.*

— Viva la / revolucion.

— Viva la revolucion.

— Money works based on agreement. And we all agree we don't want it.

— Whatever you have- trading *fruit,* whatever, whatever it is, that will eventually become the same system you destroyed.

— Not on my watch.

— But if we're all taking this pill at twenty-one, then you're dead. You've only got a few years to-

— Age corrupts.

— So what's the-

— Absolute revolution has to be absolute.

— You're such-

It doesn't matter anymore, I don't know why we're even-

— Look at the state of you. Look at that- *Look* at it!

— What?!

— Do you have some kind of syndrome? Stop *throwing* the food at them-

— I'm fine-
— Watch. Watch me. Look at that arm action. If I'm serving you your lunch, I'm *serving* you your lunch. There's commitment. Intention. You serve it looks like you have something wrong with your brain or your arm or both.
— Why's it matter?
— Oh, why's it matter? Sorry for expecting a little pride in your work. Is it too difficult feeding your comrades with essential nutrients and- She needs one, give her one.

The **Second Camper** *hands out a grenade.*

— Viva / la revolucion.
— Viva la revolucion.
— Get your act together dude, fuck. I'm embarrassed to be stood next to you.
— I'm only-

The **First Camper** *picks something out of the food, flicks it away.*

Pause.

— What was that?
— What?
— What you picked out?
— What do you think?

They serve some more.

— Well don't-
— What do you want me to do? Starve them?
— It's-
— This is lunch. Shut up and serve.

. . .

Everything changes tonight anyway.

. . .

Give him his.

The **Second Camper** *hands out a grenade.*

— Viva la rev / olucion-
— Viva la revolucion.
— You don't say it right. Say it better than that.

Nine.

TARGET.

Shooting range.
Two **Campers** *lie on their fronts. The rifles are bolted to the floor.*
They fire.
Start reloading, etc.

— Bollocks.
— It's not-
— That's not true.
— It is.
— It's obviously bollocks.
— It's not, it's true, before they, like, before *this*, before all this, they used to teach us about it in *schools*.
— You're lying.
— Some of the other kids, the older ones, the ones with parents still, they said. . .

They're aiming.

Pause.

They fire.

Start reloading, etc.

— They said the grown-ups used to teach us about sex.
— Why?
— What?
— Why would they do that?
— Because- You gotta learn about it somehow.
— What would the point be? For them, what would the point be for them.
What do they gain?

Zero for the Young Dudes! 355

— What do they gain making us do this?
— They're not *training* us to shoot are they. They're training us to shoot for *them*.
— It's just something you need to learn, it's an important thing, isn't it?
— . . .

I think they're lying to you.

— One of the older ones said that, before, they used to argue about it.

The grown-ups. It wasn't just some thing they all agreed about- Some wanted us to learn, like, really *young*. *Really* young. And then others didn't want us to learn about it at all.

— Like the army.
— I dunno.

They aim. . .

— I bet the army didn't want us to learn.

Pause.

Fire.

— Aim higher, they go down cleaner.
— If it's so important how come they don't teach us now.
— Because things are different now, they don't want us learning *now*. This was before the war and everything. Imagine if we all started doing it and having babies now.
— We still know about it though.
— Yeah, but they don't *tell* us. And they're rounding us all up and putting us in places like this, and that's *part* of it, it's not just about the war, cos I heard they've started telling the Titches all kinds of stuff about why you're not supposed to do it, and how, like, *God* and all that, and it's like the *opposite* of what it used to be. Cos if we started all doing it *now*, and having babies, and keeping the babies for ourselves, then suddenly there's this whole other group-
— An army-
— A whole other army of kids, in *waiting*, you know?

That we can say whatever we want to, and we can tell them, you know, we can teach them whatever. And make them do whatever

we *want* them to do. They want to control when we have them, and, you know, how *many* and all that.
— I dunno, that still sounds-

Another **Camper** *has sidled up, unnoticed.*

— Hey.
— Oh-
— Don't look at me, they're looking, don't look at me.
— Soz-

They pretend to aim.

The **Third Camper** *looks around for safety.*

— There's a full dorm inspection at ten fifteen.
— Ten fifteen?
— Ten fifteen, you deaf? Be ready at ten fifteen.
— Al*right*.
— Don't be a dick.

They go back to actually aiming.

Pause.

— You're the dick.

He leaves.

Fire.

— I forgot what I was even-
— Sex.
— Oh yeah, well, apparently they did anyway.
— How do you even teach it?
— I dunno. . .
— Maybe they got to watch porn.
— What's porn?
— It's videos of people doing it.
— Oh right, yeah. Well. I guess so.
How else do you learn 'cept by watching?

They take aim. . .

— Apparently everyone used to watch porn. Even grown-ups.

Pause.

Fire.

— *Shit*-
— Fucking hell, you *scalped* him.

. . .
His head looks like a yoghurt lid.
— (*From off.*) Nice job, dickhead.
— He's wriggling all over the place.
— I'm gonna finish him-
— No, you can't, don't. They don't let you do that. Just wait. You just have to wait.

They watch impassively as the target writhes and kicks.

— Look at him go.

He takes a while to bleed out.

Pause.

— . . .
— Yeah, that was a mess.

Ten.
REVISE.

In class, **Campers** *are silently copying something from one piece of paper to another.*

Time passes.

— Psst.

Pause.

— Pss-
— What?
— I'm new.

Pause.

— I'm new-
— So?
— So I don't-
— Sh / hh-
— Shut the fuck up-

She leans in.

— I don't get this.

Pause.

— I don't get-
— Get what?
— I don't get what /we're-
— Shut up-
— You just copy it out.
— Yeah, but-
— You just copy it out again.

Pause.

— It's not true though.

Pause.

— It's not-
— *What?*
— Do you have the same as me, cos mine says-
'After a fourteen-day stand-off a battalion under the order of General Hallmayne stormed the power station outside of Birmingham and freed the hos / tages-'
— Shut / up-
— Be quiet-
— . . .

(*Quieter.*) 'And freed the hostages who had suffered unthinkable torture at the hands of the Youth Rebels. After a vicious firefight with major casualties on both sides, the stranglehold placed over the city's power by the Rebels was removed, and the station was reclaimed and reactivated, continuing to fuel our homes and businesses today.'

Beat.

— So?
— But-
I was there. We didn't have any hostages. And we held the plant for like a *month*.
— So what?
— So why do we have to write it out if it's not true.
— Are you really that thick?
— I-
— Shut your fucking mouth.

Beat.

— But it's not what happened-
— Why do I-
— Just copy it out, you're supposed to have twenty copies by three-
— . . .
— Copy it *out*.

Pause.

She goes to stand up-

The **Second Camper** *yanks her back into her seat.*

— If you question it, they'll put you out on the firing range-
— It's a *lie*.
— It's *all* lies. They beat us, they get to write whatever they want.
— They'll make the Titches read it-
— Not after tonight.

...
Alright?

Pause.

They go back to writing.

Time passes.

Someone farts.

A low chuckle.

Eleven.
[EDIT].

Dear Mum,

I am having a really [GOOD] time at camp. The counsellors are all [FAIR] and one of them told me [I AM MAKING PROGRESS]. I'm sure learning a lot about [SOCIETY] and [ORDER]. There is a lot of time to [DEVELOP MYSELF] in here.

I have [LOTS OF NEW RESPONSIBILITIES], and in [LESSONS] we get to [SWIM] in the lake and [LONG DIVISION] and sometimes we [LEARN PRACTICAL SKILLS].

Don't [WORRY ABOUT ME].

If they decide [I HAVE ACHIEVED MY PERSONAL DEVELOPMENT GOALS], then know that [I AM THANKFUL TO THE CAMP AND ITS COUNSELLORS]. And that everything [I WRONGLY BELIEVED BEFORE] has [PASSED] into [INSIGNIFICANCE] and I am ready [TO BECOME A PRODUCTIVE MEMBER OF SOCIETY].

All my [RESPECT],

[YOUR SON].

Twelve.

SWALLOW.

A group of **Campers** *sit eating dinner from trays. Occasionally another will sit down and join the conversation.*

— What about Leicester?
— Yep.

Pause.

— What about Leeds?
— Mm-hm.

Pause.

— What about Birmingham?
— Yep.

Pause.

— What / about-
— What about Sheffield?
— (*Nods.*)
— What about Reading?
— Yeah.
— What about Nottingham though?
— Yes.

Pause.

— Derby?
— (*Nods.*)
— Liverpool.
— Yeah.
— Ipswich?
— Yes.
— Bristol?
— Yes.

Pause.

— Wolverhampton?
— Yes.
— Brighton?
— Yes.
— Harrogate.
— Yes.
— Halifax.
— Yes.
— Oxford.
— Yes.
— Cambridge.
— Yes.
— Durham.
— Yes.
— What about Scotland though?
— Scotland too.
— Glasgow?
— (*Nods.*)
— Edinburgh-
— Yes.
— Inverness.
— Yes-
— Middlesbrough.
— / Y-
— Middlesbrough's not in Scotland.
— No, but-
— Yes, Middlesbrough too.
— The Isle of Man?
— Yes, everything, yes. They're *all-*
— The Titches-
— The Titches too, they're just the same-
— Ireland-
— Ireland.
— Wales-
— *Yes.* Cardiff, Swansea, they're all-
— At ten fifteen.
— At ten fifteen. Everyone is ready for ten fifteen, so just. . .

Don't worry about it.
Alright?

Pause.

— What about London?
— There's no kids in London, bell-end.
— They'll *hear* it in London. They'll know it's all happening.
— How come it's all the same time?
— That's the whole point.
— But what if they don't have a dorm inspection then?
— / Everyone has an inspection at the same time, their orders are all centralised.
— They all do.
— It's so they can move us from camp to camp easier.
— She never went to another.
— You just went here?
— I'm new.
— Yeah, but, not new to-
— This isn't your first camp though.
— If it was you'd have been here ages.
— I don't, I mean. . .

Beat.

— What?
— . . . my-
my parents kept me hid.
— / For fuck's sake-
— / (*Shakes head.*)
— / Why do we always get sat with these ones-
— Calm down, she still fought. You fought, didn't you?
— I, yeah, I mean-
— Where.
— I did-
— Tell us where.
— . . .
— She's lying.
— I'm not lying, I did.

— So where then.
— . . .Marston Moor.
— / See?
— Me too.
— She's lying.
— Course she's lying.
— Why would she lie?
— She says Marston Moor cos it was so big no one can check.
— I was there-
— Everyone was there. Except her.
— My parents live in York-
— So you just stepped outside to join in then ran home afterwards?
— / No. . .
— Leave her alone.
— Why?
— She's / here now, isn't she?
— Some people had different situations-
— Her situation is that she's a pussy. Let me feel your hands.
— Why?
— I want to feel them-
— Don't listen to him.
— I want to see if they feel like our hands, or if they feel like soft coward's hands.
— / Bit harsh.
— Don't be a dick-
— She didn't fight for tomorrow!
. . .
We're all here-
We're all *meant* to be here, in their eyes.
We gave them *reasons* to lock us up.
. . .
. . .
I fought at Marston Moor.
I did.
And so did thousands of us.

So did kids six-seven years old.

...

I took down three power stations, and closed *six* schools.
I held my friends as they bled out in the streets.
They all fought and died because they believed in taking what was ours by birthright, before *they* used all of it up.
Before there was nothing left to inherit.

...

We rose up and fought for our home.
This country. This planet.
Clean air. Housing for everyone. Free healthcare. Equality.
No money. No ownership.
A tomorrow for all of us.
We did all that for *you*. While you sat in your house with your parents, content with whatever scraps they threw you.

...

I should tell them- I should tell all of them they're wasting time on you, they don't need to force you into anything- you were never on our side in the first place.
I bet you still *write* to them, don't you.
Don't you?
— ...we're allowed...
— I don't care about what they *allow* us to do.

...

When the war started I burned my parents' house to the ground.

...

We gathered in the streets.
We tore down the town hall.
The museum.
Schools.
Everything.
Smashed it to pieces.
Nothing left standing.
Everything they thought was firmly in their grasp we destroyed, because
If you butcher my future, I will massacre your past.

Pause.

— I didn't mean to-
— You didn't fight at Marston Moor.
— I-
— Did you.
— . . .
. . .
no.
. . .

Pause.

His point proven, he goes back to his food.

— You make it up to us tonight.

Thirteen.
HOLD.

Night has fallen.
Outside, round the back of one of the dorms, under a dim light, a **Camper** *stands waiting.*

Time passes.

Eventually another **Camper** *hurries on.*
Very out of breath.

— Hey.
— I nearly left.
— I couldn't-
I couldn't get away-
they were marching us-
one of the guys in my unit did something, so they were marching us-
and I couldn't get away.
. . .
I didn't think I was ever gonna get away, I thought they were just gonna march me to my dorm and then I wouldn't- But they stopped eventually.

— And you're here.
— I'm here.
— Made it.
— Yeah.
Just.
...sweating...

She catches her breath.

— I can't stay long.
— No.
— Cos of, well. You know. What we all-
— Ten fifteen.
— Yeah.
— Not long.
— Yeah.
. . .
Nervous!
. . .

Pause.

— I thought cos of- You know. I wanted to try this.
. . .
I thought, I thought I'd try it.
And I nearly missed you!
— Nearly.
— Yeah. Phew. Haha.
— (*Smiles.*)

Pause.

— Do you want to start?
— Oh, yeah. Yes. I mean- I can't stay long, so we, like we said, so. Yeah.
Have you done this before? I mean, duh, course, course you have. Stupid.

. . .
I don't know how to, um, start, so-
— Relax.
— Relax, yeah, yes.
— Just relax, and-

Voices or vehicle noise nearby. They freeze until it passes.

— Close.
— Just relax.
. . .
Breathe in through your nose like this. . .
— . . .
— . . . and then out through your mouth like this. . .
— . . .
— Just keep going like that till you feel relaxed.

They breathe for a while while looking at each other.

— And now I'll start by just getting closer to you.
— . . .
— Really close, okay?
— Oh-

She flinches a little.

— S'alright, just relax.
— . . .
— There, see.
. . .
Just keep breathing.

She stands very close. They breathe together.

— . . .
— And I'm going to put my head on your shoulder and you put yours on mine.
— . . .

They gradually come to rest their heads on each other's shoulders.

— . . .
— And then the last bit is just. . .

She brings her arms up to embrace her, closing the hug.

Pause.

The **Second Camper** *raises her arms awkwardly and hugs back.*

Pause.

— This is it?
— This is it.
— . . .

Pause.

— What do we do now?
— We just stay like this for a while.

Pause.

They separate.

— There.
— That's it?
— That's it.
— . . .
— We can do it for longer if you want.
— . . .Nah. That's alright.
— Okay.
— It was pretty good I guess.
— It's nice.
— Yeah. Nice. I guess.
I dunno. . .
. . .
. . .
. . .
Are you scared about tonight?
— No.
— No.
. . .

Me either.
— We have to take our own tomorrow or they'll force us into theirs.
— Yeah. . .

Pause.

— I better go.
— Alright.
— I'll see you anyway.
— Okay.
La tierra es vuestra.
— La tierra es vuestra.

Beat.

She leaves.

Fourteen.

CLEAN.

In pyjamas and dressing gowns, the **Campers** *play a spirited and chaotic game of Blind Man's Buff, a giggling* **Camper** *stumbling around the washroom with his dressing gown/pyjama top pulled over his head.*

Others watch while brushing teeth, yelling, mouths foaming with toothpaste.

The game should be played for real, at length.
Lots of laughter, shouts and calls, lots of improvising.

Sometimes the game tumbles into playfighting or wrestling, **Campers** *squirming on the floor in laughter, dogpiling each other, splashing water.*

At a peak of excitement, chaos and laughter, a **Camper** *walks in briskly, heading straight for a sink.*

His arms and torso are coated in blood, his clothes soaked in it.

The energy of the room gradually calms as the **Campers** *all notice their bloodied room-mate frantically washing himself.*

They watch him for a while in silence.

Eventually, one of the **Campers** *goes over and helps him wash.*

One
By
One

They all walk over and
help wash the blood away.

Fifteen.

HOME.

Dear Mum,

I am having a really good time at camp. The counsellors are all fair with me and one of them told me I am a good worker. I'm sure learning a lot about the war and my part in it. There is a lot of time to think about things in here.

I have made lots of new friends too, and in our free time we get to swim in the lake and play sports and sometimes we hear stories about how things were before.

Don't worry about me.

If they decide it's better for everyone if I never see you again, then know that I was okay in here. And that everything I ever did to you through anger has drifted out of me into dust and nothingness and I am ready for a tomorrow that can be better for all of us.

All my love,

Shelby.

Sixteen.

OUT.

The **Campers** *are hurrying to their beds-*

— Hurry up, hurry up-
— Quick, come on-
— Hurry *up-*

They all stand on their beds and look to the door.

The clock above is almost at 10:15.

They watch it tick.

Someone giggles.

— /Shhh-
— Shut up, you'll ruin it-

They watch the clock.

Seconds pass.

— Ready-

In unison, the **Campers** *all pull their grenades from under their mattresses.*

They hold them as if ready to throw.

Seconds pass.

— Pull-

In unison, the **Campers** *all pull their pins.*

The second hand begins to creep towards twelve.
The yells begin-

— La propriete, c'est le vol!
— (*All.*) Property is theft!
— La propriete, c'est le vol!
— (*All.*) Property is theft!
— Tear down fences!

— (*All.*) Burn down walls!
— Tear down fences!
— (*All.*) Burn down walls!

Perhaps we can hear the approach of **Guards**.

— One future!
— (*All.*) Our future!
— One future!
— (*All.*) Our future!
— Seize tomorrow!
— (*All.*) Destroy the past!
— Seize tomorrow!
— (*All.*) Destroy the past!
— A new nation!
— (*All.*) Conceived in liberty!

Footsteps near-
The clock hits 10:15.

— This land is yours-
— (*All.*) This land is ours!

In unison the levers of their grenades are loosed-

Each **Camper** *stuffs his or her grenade into their mouth-*

The doors begin to open-

Black.